RESUMES
THAT GET
JOBS

ACKNOWLEDGMENTS

Thanks are due to a number of people who have made substantial contributions to this new, and completely revised, seventh edition of *Resumes That Get Jobs*. Linda Bernbach, Executive Editor of Arco Publishing, provided opportunity, encouragement, and advice. Janet Stumper turned my words into a book with her graphic design skills. Jennifer Manlowe and Marty Smith graciously typed dozens of resumes. Art Ungar, of Success Strategies in Lawrenceville, New Jersey, and Marilyn Silverman, of Word Center Printing in Hamilton Square, New Jersey, shared their expertise in resume preparation. John Nebesney drew the witty illustrations with good humor of his own.

Most of all, my thanks to Saundra Young and Travis Potter for their understanding, patience, and love.

Ray Potter
Hopewell, New Jersey

IN THE SECTION MARKED "PERSONAL" BRUCE HAD WRITTEN
"SINGLE WHITE MALE SEEKS WARM, LOVING PARTNER."

RESUMES
THAT GET
JOBS

Jean Reed

Revised and expanded by
Ray Potter

Prentice Hall
New York • London • Toronto • Sydney • Tokyo • Singapore

Dedicated to Saundra and Travis with love and gratitude

Seventh Edition

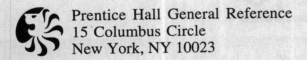

Prentice Hall General Reference
15 Columbus Circle
New York, NY 10023

Copyright © 1994 by Arco Publishing, a division
of Simon & Schuster, Inc.

An Arco Book

ARCO and PRENTICE HALL are registered trademarks of Prentice-Hall, Inc.
Colophon is a trademark of Prentice-Hall, Inc.

ISBN 0-671-86404-1

Manufactured in the United States of America

1   2   3   4   5   6   7   8   9   10

PREFACE

WHAT THIS BOOK CAN DO FOR YOU

All resumes are not equal. Some are simply better than others. This doesn't have anything to do with the backgrounds that are described on them or the talents of the people who wrote them. It's just that some resumes get attention. They communicate with potential employers. They speak directly to the needs of the people doing the hiring. This book can teach you how to write that kind of resume —resumes that get jobs. Step by step, you will learn how to write the best resume for the job you want. It's surprisingly easy. It's not painful or mysterious or filled with drudgery. You might even enjoy it!

Not all resume-writing books are equal either. Most of them are terribly out of date. The resumes they produce seem old-fashioned in today's job market. They make the people who write them seem old-fashioned too. Many resume-writing books seem almost interchangeable. They offer the same old advice that they did twenty years ago. That advice isn't going to land you a job today.

Job seekers today need every advantage they can get. Finding a job is an incredibly competitive process. Your resume can help you stand out from the competition—not by being overly flashy or garish, but by meeting the needs of the person who is looking for help. It can help you get a foot in the door, one step ahead of your competitors. This is the kind of resume that you can write with a little help from this book. You will be pleased with the resume you create—and so will your future employer.

Everything you need to prepare your resume is included in this book. There are clear instructions, worksheets for each step along the way, and even lists of words you can use that have real impact with prospective employers. Just as importantly, the whole approach described here reflects the latest techniques of market research. It will help you write a resume that incorporates the same kind of strategic planning that the most successful multinational corporations use to sell their products. After all, that's exactly what you want to do with your own resume—sell a product that you know better than anyone else: yourself.

The best person to "market" you is you. You have a thorough and intimate knowledge of your "product." You know its capabilities and its potential. You know where and how it performs best. And your "product" is unique. No one else has exactly your qualifications, your experience, your skills, your background. Whether you are entering the job market for the first time, changing jobs, switching career fields, or reentering the job market after an absence, with the guidance you find in this book you can become a successful marketer—of yourself. You can sell yourself into a job.

Let's get started!

LISA GOT A BETTER PRICE FROM THE RESUME SERVICE
BY USING ITS LETTERHEAD.

TABLE OF CONTENTS

INTRODUCTION

WHAT IS A RESUME?

A resume is a selected summary of significant facts about you. Take a minute to look at the key words in that statement. A resume doesn't present everything there is to know about you. It presents selected significant facts and it serves them up in a neatly packaged summary. To write a resume, then, you need to know which facts about you are significant to a prospective employer. You need to know how to summarize them so that your next employer can see quickly why you are the right person for the job. And you need to know how to present them on paper.

Sounds pretty simple, right? Well, it is. There are only two things you have to know to write a great resume: yourself and your future employer. If you know yourself (and who doesn't?), you're halfway there. If you know your prospective employer (and you will soon, if you don't already), you can write a resume that will get noticed.

WHAT DO RESUMES DO?

Strictly speaking, resumes don't get jobs. Resumes get interviews. And interviews get jobs. You won't get an interview without a resume. And you won't get a job offer without an interview. But the resume is the first step to a job.

Resumes save employers the time and trouble of meeting everyone who is interested in working for them. Instead of meeting face to face, they "meet" on paper. Since you don't get to talk at this first "meeting" (you're not even there!), your resume has to answer the kinds of questions that employers ask as they look over resumes. Can this person do the job? Can this person make a contribution beyond just "doing the job"? Is this person qualified? What kind of person is this applicant? (There are many more questions, but you get the idea.)

Resumes can't answer every question that employers have. If they could, there would be no need for interviews. However, the resumes that can answer the most questions, and answer them positively, are those that are going to make it to the pile marked "INTERVIEW." You have probably heard that employers who are looking through resumes sort them into three piles: NO (also known as "The Rejects Pile"); MAYBE (to be looked over again if there aren't enough resumes in the next pile); and YES (the resumes that are marked "INTERVIEW"). What you've heard is true; that's exactly how it usually works. Your goal, obviously, is to get your resume into the "YES" pile and be invited in for an interview.

A successful resume is one that leads to interviews. Interviews lead directly to jobs. Writing your resume is the first—and most important—step you can take toward getting a job. It is worth doing well because the reward is so big. Do a great job on your resume and it can lead you to a great job!

ANYONE CAN WRITE A RESUME

You don't have to be a terrific writer to write a terrific resume. Terrific writers write books. Anyone can write a resume. And it seems like everyone needs a resume today. In the sample resumes at the back of this book you will find resumes from electricians, police officers, secretaries, teachers, lawyers, counselors, and business executives—and many, many more. Most of these people wrote their resumes themselves (some of them had a little help from the author). None of them was a wonderful writer. None of them had some sort of special talent for writing resumes. They were people, just like you, who needed resumes. They wrote theirs—and you can write yours. All you need is this book and a pencil. It really is that easy.

So grab a pencil and you're on your way.

1 KNOW YOURSELF
YOUR PERSONAL SKILLS

We promised that *Resumes That Get Jobs* would take you step by step through the process of creating your own best resume. We also stated that there were only two things that you needed to know to write your best resume. The first one is: know yourself. That's where we're going to start. Here you will begin to answer the question that is always in the front of every employer's mind: "What can this person do for me?"

Like many of the sections that follow, this first chapter includes easy-to-use worksheets. After you read the brief text in each section, fill out the worksheets. These worksheets are the "building blocks" of your resume. When you have completed the worksheets you will be ready to start "constructing" your resume. This building-block approach will make it possible for you to assemble resumes for yourself—not just one resume, but a different resume every time you need a new one. It's a very flexible system, and it's very simple too. (If you have borrowed this book from a library or from a friend, you should photocopy the worksheets and write on the copies. Better yet, buy a copy of the book for yourself and then you can write in it as much as you want to!)

THE IMPORTANCE OF KNOWING YOURSELF

The most important information you need to build your resume is knowledge about what you have to offer to an employer. In the past, resumes reported only on-the-job experience. This approach helped those people who had been employed already and who were planning to take another step on the same career path. Everybody else—those who were looking for a first job, those who were reentering the workforce, those who were trying to change careers, those trying to leap up the corporate ladder without climbing it rung by rung, and many others—was hurt by this working-experience approach to resumes. From the viewpoint of employers, the jobs-only emphasis wasn't all that useful either.

What employers learned from traditional resumes was only what an applicant had done in the past and not what that applicant could do in the future.

Employers have always known that some of their best employees have been people whose past experiences didn't lead them very directly to their current positions. But they have also been afraid to take chances in hiring new employees who haven't already performed exactly the same job somewhere else. Even the most open-minded employer hasn't known how to spot potentially great employees who might have the skills to do a job but lack the direct experience.

Resume writing styles haven't helped. Most resumes today look a lot like resumes from thirty years ago. The world of work has changed a lot in the last thirty years, but you wouldn't know it to look at most resumes. And employers are still left trying to guess what the people behind these resumes have to offer.

This is one of the many places where this book is different. It begins by helping you to analyze your skills. As you will discover, skills are one of the "bridges" that allow you to cross from one type of job—even one type of career—to another.

GETTING TO KNOW YOUR SKILLS

You may not know it right now, but you have a unique set of skills. You have acquired them in every activity in which you have ever participated. Not all skills come from your past jobs (although you may have plenty of job skills as well). You have collected skills in volunteer work, in working at home, in being a student, in your hobbies, and in your extracurricular activities.

Skills are often transferable from one occupation to another. For example, teachers frequently say to career counselors: "I'm a teacher. What skills do I have besides teaching?" The answer is: "You have a lot!" And they do. Teachers have skills like time planning, motivating, supervising, setting goals, evaluating results, public speaking, and many others. So do you.

The skills worksheets that follow are designed to help you identify your particular skills. They begin by asking you to list a specific activity which has been significant to you. You can start with your most recent job or you can start with any other role that has been important for you. If you really can't think of a place to start, simply list the activity that takes up most of your time each day (besides sleeping!).

You will be asked to describe the activity. Write this description in the way you might say it to an employer if you were asked in an interview, "Tell me a little bit about that." It doesn't have to be polished or precise right now, because you will have an opportunity to rewrite it later.

NAMING YOUR SKILLS

Next you will identify the skills you used or learned in the activity you selected. Some of the skills you list are skills that you already had when you began the activity. You may have learned these in school, from a previous job, from your parents, or just from living. All of these "count" here. All are important. If you find yourself listing skills that you don't want to use on a job, drop these and concentrate on those that you would be comfortable discussing with an employer. For example, if one of your activities has been to raise a child from infancy to kindergarten, you might have acquired undeniable skills in changing diapers. However, if you are not looking for a job in child care, this is a skill that won't be much in demand. Focus instead on the time planning, household management, and related skills that you had to employ in child rearing.

Following the worksheets is a sample list of skills you can refer to after you make your own list, in case you forgot to include some of the skills you used or learned. There are three skills worksheets included. You can complete fewer than three or do more if you want (photocopy the worksheets or use your own sheets of paper if you want to analyze more than three activities).

THE SKILLS SUMMARY

After you have identified skills for your activities, you will be ready to fill out the "Skills Summary" worksheet. Here you will be asked to look over the skills that you recorded for each activity and to take a look at the sample list too. From these, you will select the personal skills that you would like a prospective employer to know you have. Don't worry now about how you will use these in your resume. That will become clear later. For now, fill out the worksheets and the summary and congratulate yourself on accomplishing a feat that few resume writers have been able to accomplish!

SKILLS WORKSHEET

Activity (This can be a job, a volunteer activity, a hobby, a project, etc.)

_____

_____

_____

_____

Description of the activity (Briefly describe what you did.)

_____

_____

_____

_____

Skills you used or learned in the activity _____

_____

_____

_____

_____

_____

_____

(Refer to the sample list of skills after you have made your own and add any from the list that you haven't included already.)

SKILLS WORKSHEET

Activity (This can be a job, a volunteer activity, a hobby, a project, etc.)

_____

_____

_____

_____

Description of the activity (Briefly describe what you did.)

_____

_____

_____

_____

Skills you used or learned in the activity _____

_____

_____

_____

_____

_____

(Refer to the sample list of skills after you have made your own and add any from the list that you haven't included already.)

SKILLS WORKSHEET

Activity (This can be a job, a volunteer activity, a hobby, a project, etc.)

_____

_____

_____

_____

Description of the activity (Briefly describe what you did.)

_____

_____

_____

_____

Skills you used or learned in the activity _____

_____

_____

_____

_____

_____

_____

(Refer to the sample list of skills after you have made your own and add any from the list that you haven't included already.)

SAMPLE LIST OF SKILLS

You use skills and learn skills in every activity, whether it is a job, a hobby, a volunteer position, or working around the house or apartment. Usually you can identify your skills just by concentrating on the activity and thinking about the skills that it required. This sample list is included here to stimulate your thinking. It doesn't pretend to be comprehensive, but it should trigger your thoughts as you analyze your activities. Refer to this list as you complete the Skills Worksheets and the Skills Summary.

Planning	Supervising
Leading	Coordinating
Communicating	Analyzing
Persuading	Selling
Coaching	Counseling
Teaching	Instructing
Solving problems	Finding solutions
Resolving conflicts	Keeping records
Motivating	Mediating
Writing	Explaining
Creating	Innovating
Attending to details	Decision making
Budgeting	Bookkeeping
Managing time	Tracking details
Increasing productivity	Increasing profit
Stimulating growth	Stimulating sales

SKILLS SUMMARY

From the skills you identified on the skills worksheets and from the sample list of skills, note below those skills that you would like a prospective employer to know you have. For each skill that you include, ask yourself one question: Will I be comfortable talking with a future employer about this? If the answer is no, drop it from your list of skills. If you're not sure about the answer to the question, leave it on your list for now.

1. _____

2. _____

3. _____

4. _____

5. _____

6. _____

7. _____

8. _____

9. _____

10. _____

2 KNOWING EVEN MORE
YOUR PERSONAL QUALIFICATIONS

Congratulations! You have completed the first step in creating your own best resume! Now it's time to move on to the next chapter and explore your "Personal Qualifications."

Just as you have a unique collection of skills, you have your own set of personal qualifications. People often refer to their qualifications as "aspects of my personality." You might say: "That's just who I am." Well, who are you? That's what you need to put down on paper under the heading of personal qualifications. Look at this as if you were someone else—maybe your best friend—describing you. What would you say?

Personal qualifications are sometimes called "traits" or "qualities." They are usually best described with short phrases, like: quick learner; good with my hands; can talk to just about anybody; pleasant personality; always keep cool under pressure; able to do many things at once, etc. Don't think of these only as job related. You are trying to describe yourself to someone who has never met you. You're creating a "word picture" of yourself.

Of course, you're trying to emphasize the positive here. You can leave out the negative aspects of your personality. This is not the place to note, for example, "I'm a real hothead" or "I drive people nuts with my constant talking." These may be aspects of your personality, but they're not what we're looking for here!

If you find it difficult to describe your personal qualifications, even after you have tried to look at yourself as your best friend might look at you, it's time to ask your best friend for help. Ask that friend (better yet, ask two or three) to describe your best qualities. Take notes while your friend is talking and then transfer your notes to the worksheet. (After all, what are friends for if not to tell you what they think is best about you?) There is a list of sample personal qualifications right after the worksheet, in case you want to add to your list. But don't go right to this sample list. You (and your best friend) can describe you much better than the list can.

PERSONAL QUALIFICATIONS WORKSHEET

What are your best personal qualities? (Briefly describe them with a word or a phrase.)

1. _____

2. _____

3. _____

4. _____

5. _____

6. _____

7. _____

8. _____

9. _____

10. _____

(Refer to the sample list after you have made your own and add any from that list that you haven't included already.)

Congratulations! You have completed the second step in creating your own best resume! Now it's time to move on to the next section.

PERSONAL QUALIFICATIONS

The descriptive words below are only a sample of the kinds of words you might use to describe yourself. They can be used to trigger your own thoughts about your best qualities. Refer to this list when you are filling out your Personal Qualifications Worksheet.

Reliable	Dependable
Well-organized	Quick learner
Self-motivated	Self-starter
Imaginative	Bright
Smart	Intelligent
Thorough	Conscientious
Persuasive	Diplomatic
Friendly	Outgoing
Loyal	Persistent
Practical	Problem-solver
Active	Calm
Trustworthy	Inquisitive
Dedicated	Giving
Methodical	Productive
Creative	Ingenious
Clever	Original
Systematic	Businesslike
Professional	Honest

Unique	Skilled
Talented	Adept
Able	Competent
Efficient	Proficient
Exceptional	Congenial
Devoted	Energetic
Aggressive	Assertive
Genial	Gregarious
Truthful	Composed
Patient	Tenacious
Poised	Even-tempered
Astute	Incisive
Perceptive	Rational
Curious	Discerning
Sensible	Thoughtful
Precise	Flexible
Insightful	Caring
Versatile	Responsible
Analytic	Organized

3 "WORK EXPERIENCE"

DESCRIBING YOUR "WORK"

Once you have completed the Personal Skills Worksheets, the Skills Summary, and the Personal Qualifications Worksheet, you have put part of yourself down on paper. Let's call that the "personal part" of you. Now it's time to turn your attention to what we might call the "public part" of you. This is where you get to describe your experience in specific jobs—or in other positions of responsibility. Actually, you have already started this process by identifying "activities" when you filled out your Personal Skills Worksheets. You will start in a similar way here.

"WORK EXPERIENCE"

"Work experience" is in quotation marks because the name isn't exactly right. What we're actually talking about here is just "experience," but not every experience you have had in your life. In this section, you will focus on your experiences that are "work-like," whether or not you actually got paid or had a formal job. These may be the experiences that gave you some of the "personal skills" you have already recorded—the experiences that we called "activities" in the section where you analyzed your skills.

Completing the "Work Experience" Worksheets is a three-stage process. First you will describe the experience; then you will add "action words"; and, finally, you will put in "facts and figures." With each "Work Experience" Worksheet you complete, you will have added another "building block" for constructing your resume.

If you have held jobs, you will probably want to use those jobs—and job titles—on your "Work Experience" worksheets. If you have not worked (or haven't worked in the last ten years or more), you will want to use the kind of experience you used on your Skills Worksheet: a volunteer or unpaid position, a part-time job, a summer job, an internship or "co-op" position, a job in the home, etc. In fact, if you have held a responsible position as a volunteer, you may want to add this to your list of experiences even if you have been employed at a full-time job as well. Employers like to know what people do outside their jobs; if you have been able to hold a significant volunteer position, it says something positive about you.

The "Work Experience" Worksheets are easy to use. First, fill in the top of the form. Start with your present job or position on the first worksheet and then work backwards chronologically through your previous jobs or activities. List the main responsibilities of your position next to the numbers. Begin with your most important responsibility next to number one and work down in priority if you can. (If you can't put your responsibilities into a ranked order very easily, don't worry about it. Any order is fine for now.)

ADDING "ACTION WORDS"

Once you have recorded the key tasks of your position, use the next section of the form to re-word these tasks so that they include action words. These are essential to the success of your resume. Ideally, the descriptions of your positions will consist of short phrases that each begin with an action word. There is a list of sample action words at the end of the "Work Experience" Worksheets. You can take words from this list or use your own words. The secrets here are to keep the phrases brief and the first words "strong."

For example, you might have said in the first section of the worksheet: "As the assistant to the purchasing manager, I make sure that bid forms go out to possible vendors and then I record the bids when they come back in. I have an assistant who takes care of the filing and the mailing." Now you are going to transform those statements by shortening them and using action words. Your new description might come out like this: "Coordinate bid process. Identify vendors. Send bid forms. Track responses. Supervise filing and mailing staff."

You can do this for any responsibilities and for any jobs. It's not hard to do. Just use the action words list and cut out any unnecessary words. This has two important results. First, it makes your descriptions easy for prospective employers to read and to understand. Second, it commands attention. This is the kind of "no nonsense" approach that gets results.

ADDING "FACTS AND FIGURES"

Your last step in perfecting the descriptions of your work experience is to add "facts and figures." This is where you make your job or activity as concrete as possible. The questions to answer here are "How many?" "How much time?" "For whom?" "With what results?" There may be others that apply to your position. In the example we used above, we might add: "Contact approximately 250 vendors a year. Process bids in excess of $500,000 a year. File more than 2000 pages per year. Handle more than 30 phone calls a day for the purchasing department."

Again, you can do this for any job. It requires some estimating on your part, but no one knows your responsibilities better than you do. You will probably be surprised at the numbers you can add here. This information makes your job more "real" to prospective employers and makes you more appealing as a candidate. It is an extremely useful addition to your resume.

The three-part process you will use to fill out the "Work Experience" Worksheets is crucial for your resume. Be sure to finish all three steps for each "experience." There are three worksheets included at the end of this section. If you need more than three, photocopy the worksheet or use separate sheets of paper and follow the same process.

WORK EXPERIENCE WORKSHEET

Job title (or position held) _____

Employer (company, agency, etc.) _____

Dates: From_____ (month/year)

To _____ (month/year)

Briefly describe employer _____
_____

Responsibilities (Describe what you did in this job or activity. Put the most important responsibilities first if you can.)

1.

2.

3.

Add "action words." Restate each of the responsibilities you listed above, but make each statement as brief as possible and begin each with an action word.

1.

2.

3.

Add "facts and figures." You can either rewrite your statements from the section above with numbers, dollars, etc., or make a separate list.

1.

2.

3.

WORK EXPERIENCE WORKSHEET

Job title (or position held) _____

Employer (company, agency, etc.) _____

Dates: From_____ (month/year)

To _____ (month/year)

Briefly describe employer _____
_____

Responsibilities (Describe what you did in this job or activity. Put the most important responsibilities first if you can.)

1.

2.

3.

Add "action words." Restate each of the responsibilities you listed above, but make each statement as brief as possible and begin each with an action word.

1.

2.

3.

Add "facts and figures." You can either rewrite your statements from the section above with numbers, dollars, etc., or make a separate list.

1.

2.

3.

WORK EXPERIENCE WORKSHEET

Job title (or position held) _____

Employer (company, agency, etc.) _____

Dates: From_____ (month/year)

To _____ (month/year)

Briefly describe employer_____
_____

Responsibilities (Describe what you did in this job or activity. Put the most important responsibilities first if you can.)

1.

2.

3.

Add "action words." Restate each of the responsibilities you listed above, but make each statement as brief as possible and begin each with an action word.

1.

2.

3.

Add "facts and figures." You can either rewrite your statements from the section above with numbers, dollars, etc., or make a separate list.

1.

2.

3.

"ACTION WORDS"

To communicate quickly and powerfully with prospective employers, use "action" words wherever you can on your resume (and in your cover letter too). This list will provide you with suggestions, but it should not confine you. If you have a better word, use it. Take a look at the sample resumes at the back of the book to see how other job seekers have used "action words" in their resumes.

Developed	Initiated	Coordinated
Controlled	Advised	Authored
Performed	Implemented	Recommended
Designed	Maintained	Analyzed
Operated	Explained	Reviewed
Monitored	Suggested	Compiled
Generated	Adjusted	Produced
Revised	Created	Adapted
Supervised	Instructed	Planned
Enhanced	Built	Modified
Wrote	Reported	Determined
Debugged	Organized	Augmented
Conceived	Acquired	Purchased
Executed	Managed	Proposed
Assisted	Negotiated	Evaluated
Corresponded	Trained	Streamlined
Documented	Provided	Persuaded

Promoted	Improved	Examined
Simplified	Invented	Engineered
Arranged	Contacted	Packaged
Recognized	Programmed	Collected
Placed	Prepared	Saved
Investigated	Taught	Coached
Researched	Discovered	Counseled
Assembled	Constructed	Estimated
Installed	Repaired	Screened
Dispatched	Inspected	Audited
Budgeted	Cultivated	Tested
Appraised	Manufactured	Elicited
Lectured	Lobbied	Advertised
Interviewed	Hired	Fired
Logged	Catalogued	Copyrighted
Patented	Inventoried	Posted
Edited	Balance	Steered
Vended	Translated	Transcribed
Rescued	Displayed	Took part in
Closed (a deal)	Was in charge of	Was responsible for
Accomplished	Presented	Completed
Reorganized	Identified	Delivered

Restored	Instituted	Diagnosed
Sold	Made	Guided
Founded	Approved	Administered
Replaced	Increased	Established
Expanded	Calculated	Directed
Supplied	Produced	Headed
Interpreted	Represented	Scheduled
Distributed	Achieved	Conducted
Obtained	Selected	Referred
Formulated	Enlarged	Motivated
Devised	Solved	Studied
Ordered	Led	Consolidated
Eliminated	Decreased	Designated
Reduced	Processed	Composed
Served	Disproved	Detected
Won	Merged	

DALE'S RESUME REALLY DESCRIBES HIS CAREER IN THE
RESTAURANT BUSINESS.

4 ACCOMPLISHMENTS

DESCRIBING YOUR "ACHIEVEMENTS"

Completing the Accomplishments Worksheet will make you feel good. It focuses on your personal triumphs. Here's the idea. No matter what jobs or positions you have had, you have had some "accomplishments" along the way. These may be "big deal" accomplishments—like securing a new contract worth a million dollars to your company or starting up a new branch office by yourself—or they may seem like "no big deal" to you—like reorganizing a filing system or just getting everything done on time. This is the place to jot these down. Why? Because they show initiative on your part and an awareness of the needs of your employer. They show the *contributions* you have made in the past and they suggest the contributions you could make in the future. Remember, this is the kind of information that employers want but rarely find on resumes.

Staying with the example we used in the previous chapter, our assistant to the purchasing manager might fill out the Accomplishments Worksheet like this: "Streamlined purchasing process, saving the company time and paper. Started first computerized tracking process, making it possible to check the status of any vendor or bid. Found approximately 45 new vendors, resulting in savings of more than $25,000 in first year on the job."

As you can see, "action words" and "facts and figures" are as important on the Accomplishments Worksheet as they were on the "Work Experience" Worksheets. The sheets are set up in the same way and use the same three-step process. First, note your accomplishments. Second, add action words. Third, add facts and figures. Use the same experiences for your Accomplishments Worksheets that you used on your "Work Experience" Worksheets. Remember that these can be paid or unpaid jobs, part-time jobs, summer jobs, volunteer activities, internships, jobs in the home, etc. The focus here is on what you have achieved. Remember to be as specific as possible.

ACCOMPLISHMENTS WORKSHEET

Job title (or position held) _____

Accomplishments

1.

2.

3.

Add "action words." If you haven't already included action words, rewrite the statements above to be as brief as possible and begin each with an "action word."

1.

2.

3.

Add "facts and figures." If you haven't already included the specifics of your accomplishments, do so now. Rewrite each statement so that it includes numbers, dollars, etc.

1.

2.

3.

ACCOMPLISHMENTS WORKSHEET

Job title (or position held) _____

Accomplishments

1.

2.

3.

Add "action words." If you haven't already included action words, rewrite the statements above to be as brief as possible and begin each with an "action word."

1.

2.

3.

Add "facts and figures." If you haven't already included the specifics of your accomplishments, do so now. Rewrite each statement so that it includes numbers, dollars, etc.

1.

2.

3.

ACCOMPLISHMENTS

Job title (or position held) _____

Accomplishments

1.

2.

3.

Add "action words." If you haven't already included action words, rewrite the statements above to be as brief as possible and begin each with an "action word."

1.

2.

3.

Add "facts and figures." If you haven't already included the specifics of your accomplishments, do so now. Rewrite each statement so that it includes numbers, dollars, etc.

1.

2.

3.

5 | JOB SKILLS

DESCRIBING "ON THE JOB" SKILLS

The Job Skills Worksheets are the easiest worksheets yet. This is the place you can record your skills that are directly job-related.Even if you have never held a paying job, you have job skills. Again you have to "think like an employer" and identify skills that might be needed in the kinds of jobs you want. If you have gained any of those skills from the five activities that you have analyzed in the two previous chapters, include them on the appropriate Job Skills Worksheet. Here you can note the kinds of equipment you know how to operate or the computers and software packages you know how to use. Add skills here like your proficiency in speaking or writing languages other than English. Once again, use action words and be as concrete as possible.

Our purchasing assistant might record job skills like these: "Proficient in use of WordPerfect and Xywrite word processing software. Type 75 words per minute. Regularly use Lotus 1-2-3 spreadsheet software. Speak conversational Spanish. Often draft letters for supervisor." These are the kinds of skills you have too—and this is the spot to include them. Just as before, if you can't think of the kinds of job skills you have, take a look at your job description (if you have one), your on-the-job evaluations by your supervisor, or ask a colleague. Looking through the resumes in the back of this book can also help to stimulate your creativity.

Three Job Skills Worksheets follow. Use the same three experiences here that you have used on the "Work Experience" Worksheets and the Accomplishments Worksheets. Concentrate here on "what it takes to do this job," even if the job is part-time or unpaid. You have skills that you have learned or applied in every position you have held. This is the place where you can record them.

JOB SKILLS WORKSHEET

Job title (or position held) _____

What skills did you use in this position? What skills have you learned that are directly job related?

1.

2.

3.

Add action words. If possible, use action words in describing your skills. Rewrite each skill you listed above so that it is as direct as it can be.

1.

2.

3.

Add "facts and figures." If you haven't included specifics, now is the time to add them. Rewrite each skill so that it is as "fact filled" as possible.

1.

2.

3.

JOB SKILLS WORKSHEET

Job title (or position held) _____

What skills did you use in this position? What skills have you learned that are directly job related?

1.

2.

3.

Add action words. If possible, use action words in describing your skills. Rewrite each skill you listed above so that it is as direct as it can be.

1.

2.

3.

Add "facts and figures." If you haven't included specifics, now is the time to add them. Rewrite each skill so that it is as "fact filled" as possible.

1.

2.

3.

JOB SKILLS WORKSHEET

Job title (or position held) _____

What skills did you use in this position? What skills have you learned that are directly job related?

1.

2.

3.

Add action words. If possible, use action words in describing your skills. Rewrite each skill you listed above so that it is as direct as it can be.

1.

2.

3.

Add "facts and figures." If you haven't included specifics, now is the time to add them. Rewrite each skill so that it is as "fact filled" as possible.

1.

2.

3.

6 QUALIFICATIONS SUMMARY

A CAPSULE DESCRIPTION OF YOURSELF

Now that you know your personal skills, your personal qualifications, your experiences, your accomplishments, and your "job skills," this is a good time to try to summarize them. You are going to write a "capsule description" of who you are and what you have to offer to a prospective employer. This may become the opening section of your resume or it may be included in the cover letter that accompanies your resume. (With a few modifications, it might be used in both places.)

Your goal with the "qualifications summary" is to get an employer interested in you—interested enough to want to know more. This means that you need to "think like an employer." Think about what you have to offer. Think about what will appeal to a person who is screening resumes, looking for people who might be worth interviewing.

You have already done the work for this section. Take a look back through your worksheets and see what stands out to you. It's fine to steal from what you have already written. Your Skills Worksheet is a good place to start. Maybe you will find some key words in your Personal Qualifications Worksheet that show what you have to contribute. Perhaps you have some specific "work experiences" that should be highlighted so they can't be missed. Maybe it's an accomplishment that's so impressive it's bound to interest a prospective employer.

Just as you have done in your other worksheets, you should make sure that your summary uses brief, direct phrases and includes relevant "facts and figures." You might want to glance through the resumes at the back of the book to help formulate your description of yourself.

QUALIFICATIONS SUMMARY WORKSHEET

Who are you? What skills and qualifications do you have? What things do you want an employer to know about you? Use the spaces below to develop a brief summary of yourself.

QUALIFICATIONS SUMMARY: FIRST DRAFT

_____
_____
_____
_____
_____
_____
_____
_____
_____

QUALIFICATIONS SUMMARY: SECOND DRAFT

_____
_____
_____
_____
_____
_____
_____
_____
_____

QUALIFICATIONS SUMMARY: FINAL VERSION

_____
_____
_____
_____
_____
_____
_____
_____

7 EDUCATION

SUMMARIZING YOUR EDUCATION AND TRAINING

Employers are always interested in the education of their prospective employees. Their interest means that your resume will probably need a section that highlights your education. (There are a few exceptions to this rule that we will discuss when we bring all the pieces of the resume together, but for now you should assume that your resume will need to include your education and you should complete this section.)

The Education Worksheet that follows is pretty straightforward. You will be able to fill it out without a lot of effort. There are two identical sections for each level of your education, in case you attended more than one school or attained more than one degree at that level. This whole "building block" is fairly easy, so jump in and get started!

NOTE: IF YOUR FORMAL EDUCATION ENDED WITH HIGH SCHOOL, AND YOU HAVE BEEN OUT OF HIGH SCHOOL FOR MORE THAN FIVE YEARS, THE ONLY SECTIONS YOU NEED TO COMPLETE ARE THE LAST THREE: "VOCATIONAL OR TRADE SCHOOL," "WORK-RELATED COURSES," AND "TRAINING," IF ANY OF THESE APPLIES TO YOU.

EDUCATION WORKSHEET: HIGH SCHOOL

(NOTE: IF YOU COMPLETED TWO OR MORE YEARS OF COLLEGE, OR IF YOU ARE MORE THAN FIVE YEARS OUT OF HIGH SCHOOL, SKIP THIS SECTION.)

Name of high school _____

City and state _____

Attended from _____ to_____   Graduated _____

Grade point average _____   Rank in class _____

Honors, awards, prizes _____
_____

Special courses or programs _____

Extracurricular achievements _____

_____

Additional high school (if you attended more than one)

Name of high school _____

City and state _____

Attended from _____ to _____   Graduated _____

Grade point average _____   Rank in class (if known) _____

Honors, awards, prizes_____

Special courses or programs_____

Extracurricular achievements_____

_____

EDUCATION WORKSHEET: COLLEGE

Name of college _____

City and state _____

Attended from _____ to _____ Graduated _____

Grade point average _____ Rank in class _____

Degree _____ Major or concentration _____

Additional major or concentration _____

Honors, awards, prizes _____

Special courses or programs _____

Extracurricular achievements _____

_____

Additional college (if you attended more than one)

Name of college _____

City and state _____

Attended from _____ to_____ Graduated _____

Grade point average _____ Rank in class _____

Degree _____ Major or concentration _____

Honors, awards, prizes _____

Special courses or programs _____

Extracurricular achievements _____

_____

EDUCATION WORKSHEET: GRADUATE SCHOOL

Name of graduate school _____

City and state _____

Attended from _____ to _____

Graduated _____

Grade point average _____ Rank in class _____

Degree _____ Field of study _____

Concentrations or specialties _____

Thesis or dissertation title _____

Honors, awards, prizes _____

_____

Special courses or programs _____

Extracurricular achievements _____

_____

ADDITIONAL GRADUATE SCHOOL (if you attended more than one)

Name of graduate school _____

City and state _____

Attended from _____ to_____   Graduated _____

Grade point average _____ Rank in class_____

Degree _____ Field of study _____

Concentrations or specialties _____

Thesis or dissertation title _____

Honors, awards, prizes _____

_____

Special courses or programs _____

Extracurricular achievements _____

_____

EDUCATION WORKSHEET: VOCATIONAL OR TRADE SCHOOL

Name of school _____

City and state _____

Attended from _____ to _____ Graduated _____

Diploma or certificate earned _____

Specialty or concentration _____

Grade point average _____ Rank in class _____

Honors, awards, prizes _____

Skills learned _____

_____

Additional vocational or trade school

Name of school _____

City and state _____

Attended from _____ to _____ Graduated _____

Diploma or certificate earned _____

Specialty or concentration _____

Grade point average_____ Rank in class _____

Honors, awards, prizes _____

Skills learned _____

_____

EDUCATION WORKSHEET: WORK-RELATED COURSES

List here any courses you have taken that are job-related. These can include short courses such as workshops and seminars and longer courses, either on-the-job or in educational institutions.

Course title _____

School name _____

City and state_____

Date course was taken _____

Diploma or certificate earned _____

Honors, awards, prizes _____

_____

Skills learned _____

_____

Additional Work-Related Courses

Course title _____

School name _____

School address (city and state) _____

Date course was taken _____

Diploma or certificate earned _____

Honors, awards, prizes _____

Skills learned _____

_____

EDUCATION WORKSHEET: TRAINING

If you have received special training, either on-the-job or in an educational institution, list it here.

Special training _____

School name _____

City and state _____

Dates of training: from _____ to _____

Diploma or certificate earned _____

Honors, awards, prizes _____

_____

Skills learned _____

_____

ADDITIONAL TRAINING

Special training _____

School name _____

City and state _____

Dates of training: from _____ to _____

Diploma or certificate earned _____

Honors, awards, prizes _____

Skills learned _____

_____

8 AWARDS

RECORDING RECOGNITION

Although you might think of "awards" as something won only at lavish banquets or internationally televised celebrations, the fact is that awards are handed out regularly for all kinds of achievements. Some are work related and some are not. Any award you have won might be listed on your resume. Ideally, the awards you include will be fairly recent (within, say, the last five years), and will communicate positively to a prospective employer (even an award for "good attendance" says something positive about you).

The Awards Worksheet lets you describe the awards you may have received. The decision to include an award on your resume is yours to make (and will be discussed further when we talk about the best ways to put your resume together). For now, put down on the worksheet any award that you are willing to discuss with a potential employer.

AWARDS WORKSHEET

Award received _____

Awarding organization _____

Date of award _____

Description of award _____

_____

Award received _____

Awarding organization _____

Date of award _____

Description of award _____

_____

Award received _____

Awarding organization _____

Date of award _____

Description of award _____

_____

Award received _____

Awarding organization _____

Date of award _____

Description of award _____

_____

9 | MEMBERSHIPS

ASSOCIATIONS, CLUBS, AND ORGANIZATIONS

Your memberships in professional associations, clubs, organizations, and groups can be listed on your resume. They are most useful to you if they do any of the following: relate directly to the jobs you will be seeking; show your initiative outside your worklife—for example, a position of leadership in a volunteer role; or communicate something about you that you don't want to state directly in another part of your resume—perhaps your race, religion, ethnic background, or physical handicap.

Although your memberships can demonstrate positive qualities about you as a candidate for a job, they also offer prospective employers the chance to discriminate against you based on the stereotypes they have of the organizations you put on your resume. This is more obvious if you list an organization that usually includes only members of specific racial or religious groups, but it is true of other types of memberships as well. Remember to weigh these possibilities when you consider whether or not to include specific memberships on your resume.

Your memberships can be listed on your resume as simply the name of the organization or you can follow the name with the offices you have held, the number of years you have been a member, and even a brief description of the group itself if it is an association that is not well known. On the Memberships Worksheet, list the memberships that you consider to be the most important. For each, you can note any offices you have held or special projects you have coordinated. You can also include the length of your membership if you choose.

MEMBERSHIPS WORKSHEET

Name of organization _____

Number of years you have been a member _____

Offices held _____
(Add dates to each office if you think that these are important.)
_____
_____

Special projects (list your title if you held a position of leadership for the project)
_____
_____

Name of organization _____

Number of years you have been a member _____

Offices held _____
(Add dates to each office if you think that these are important.)
_____
_____

Special projects (list your title if you held a position of leadership for the project)
_____
_____

Name of organization _____

Number of years you have been a member _____

Offices held _____
(Add dates to each office if you think that these are important.)
_____
_____

Special projects (list your title if you held a position of leadership for the project)
_____
_____

10 PUBLICATIONS

YOUR WRITTEN WORDS

If you have written publications in the course of your work or schooling, you might want to list them in a special section of your resume. "Publications" can range from news notes printed in company newsletters to professional articles published in trade journals. If you have had your written words printed anywhere, they could be considered "publications."

You can arrange the Publications section of your resume with any structure you choose. (We will discuss this further when we describe how to assemble the resume.) The Publications Worksheet will help you organize the information you want to present. Some of your entries may contain more information than others. For now, put down all of the information that seems relevant. Note that there is space to include a description of your publication, even though this is not usually included on a resume. It's here in case you feel that the title and other information are not sufficient to describe your work. You don't have to use this section, but it's here if you need it. If you need additional worksheets, photocopy the worksheet or use a separate sheet of paper.

PUBLICATIONS WORKSHEET

Title (or brief description) of your writing_____

_____

Title (or brief description) of publication in which your writing was published

_____

Date of publication (include issue number if relevant) _____

Description of this work _____

_____

PUBLICATIONS WORKSHEET

Title (or brief description) of your writing_____

_____

Title (or brief description) of publication in which your writing was published

_____

Date of publication (include issue number if relevant) _____

Description of this work _____

_____

PUBLICATIONS WORKSHEET

Title (or brief description) of your writing_____

_____

Title (or brief description) of publication in which your writing was published

_____

Date of publication (include issue number if relevant) _____

Description of this work _____

_____

11 PERSONAL INFORMATION

USING INFORMATION TO YOUR ADVANTAGE

Once upon a time all resumes included a section that described what might be called "personal information." This section included things like marital status, number of children, church affiliation, health, etc. Today, it is against the law for employers to ask questions about race, religion, marital status, and physical handicaps (unless a handicap prevents accomplishing parts of a job). In some parts of the U.S. it is also illegal to ask about personal sexual preferences as well. And, although it is not illegal, it is considered improper for a prospective employer to ask any questions that are not directly job-related. As a consequence, "personal information" sections of resumes have largely disappeared.

However, there may be things about you that you would like an employer to know that simply don't fit into any of the categories we have covered. Examples are volunteer activities, leadership positions outside your worklife, a hobby that you are passionate about, a strong commitment to an organization or cause, etc. These can all be communicated on your resume under a heading like "personal information."

This same section can be used to relate information that an employer cannot ask, but that you may see as beneficial to your candidacy for a position. For example, if you are applying for a position where frequent out-of-town travel will be required, you might note on your resume: "Single, available to travel." (You can just as easily note that you are "Available to travel" without revealing your marital status.) Similarly, if you know that your race can be an asset in the job you are seeking, you could include it in "personal information" by stating it directly ("African-American" or "Native American," for example) or indirectly through your affiliations ("Member, Puerto Rican Action Organization").

The Personal Information Worksheet is completely optional. You don't have to fill in any information at all. If you think that there are facts about you that you would like a prospective employer to know, this is the place to include them. The topics below are only suggestions. Use the additional space at the bottom of the form to include any information that you think is important.

PERSONAL INFORMATION WORKSHEET

Social organization memberships _____
_____
_____
_____

Positions held in organizations _____
_____
_____
_____

Hobbies _____
_____
_____
_____

Awards or prizes for hobbies _____
_____
_____

Other information you might want to include on your resume _____
_____
_____
_____
_____
_____
_____
_____

12 **REFERENCES**

WHAT THEY ARE AND HOW TO USE THEM

It is not required that you include in your resume a section entitled "References." However, you may want to put one in. "References" are people who can offer comments about you to a possible employer. Sometimes references are described as either "Work References" or "Character References" (also called "Personal References"). The first group would normally include former supervisors or co-workers who can evaluate your performance as an employee. The second group would include people who can offer an appraisal of your personal qualities. (Those in this group should not be relatives, but they can be longstanding friends.)

Most employers will want to speak with a previous employer before they offer you a job. (This is referred to as "checking references.") However, in most job fields it is not common for a prospective employer to check your references before interviewing you. Because of this, it is often more useful to have a separate printed list of your references available to hand (or mail) to an interested possible employer than it is to take up space on your resume listing information that it is not actually needed.

However, having just stated a rule, let's discuss the exceptions to it. First, if you are looking for work in a field where it is common for employers to check references before they interview candidates, you obviously need to include complete information about your references directly on your resume.

The second exception to the rule: if your references are well-known people, you may want to include them even if you are pretty sure that they won't be called before you are offered an interview. Including a person who is a "big name" reflects well on you and intrigues a prospective employer. If including references on your resume increases your chances of getting an interview, then definitely include references!

HANDLING REFERENCES

1) You can simply put down "References" as a heading and then say something like "Available on request." This is frequently encountered on resumes, but it doesn't have much real value. It implies that you do have references but, frankly, your prospective employer is going to expect this anyway.

2) You can use the general heading of "References" and list one to four people who could be contacted.

3) You can distinguish between "Work References" and "Personal References," including one or two people in each category.

REFERENCES RULES

1) Be sure to talk with your references before you put their names on your resume! You must have their permission before you include their names. They must be prepared to receive a call at any time and you must be confident that they will give your prospective employer an appropriate appraisal of you.

2) Be sure to include all of the information that a prospective employer might want to know: complete titles (even for your personal references), phone numbers if your references are willing to take phone calls, and the best time to call (if your references have expressed preferences).

3) Be sure that the information is accurate and up to date. It is embarrassing (and potentially damaging to your candidacy) to have the phone number of a reference listed incorrectly or to have the title of a reference be out of date.

The References Worksheet provides space for you to write down the information you need for each of your references. If you need additional space, photocopy the worksheet or use a separate piece of paper. Even if you have decided not to include references on your resume, you should complete the worksheet because you will still need to have a list of references available for prospective employers.

REFERENCES WORKSHEET: REFERENCE #1

Name _____

Title _____

Company/organization name _____

Address (use work address unless reference wants to be contacted at home)

_____

_____

Phone _____

Best hours to call _____

Relationship to you _____

REFERENCES WORKSHEET: REFERENCE #2

Name _____

Title _____

Company/organization name _____

Address (use work address unless reference wants to be contacted at home)

_____

_____

Phone _____

Best hours to call _____

Relationship to you _____

REFERENCES WORKSHEET: REFERENCE #3

Name _____

Title _____

Company/organization name _____

Address (use work address unless reference wants to be contacted at home)

_____

_____

Phone _____

Best hours to call _____

Relationship to you _____

REFERENCES WORKSHEET: REFERENCE #4

Name _____

Title _____

Company/organization name _____

Address (use work address unless reference wants to be contacted at home)

_____

_____

Phone _____

Best hours to call _____

Relationship to you _____

13 YOUR JOB OBJECTIVE

WHAT DO YOU WANT (AND WHAT CAN YOU CONTRIBUTE)?

You may have noticed that some resumes have a "job objective" right up at the top. Some don't. It's not essential that your resume have a job objective since you will almost always mail it with a cover letter (we'll get to the cover letter later). Even if you hand it directly to a person—and don't have a cover letter—it's likely that the person will know which position you are applying for and won't have to look at the "job objective" for a reminder.

The one situation in which it is useful to have a job objective is when your objective is an exact match with the job you are seeking. This makes you look like a contender right away. If you plan to look for only one kind of position, it makes sense to include a job objective in your resume. If you are going to be applying for a variety of positions, it makes more sense to include a "Qualifications Summary" (like the one you wrote earlier). We'll discuss this further when we talk about assembling your resume.

If you think that you will be applying for two or three different kinds of jobs and you plan to have a different resume for each type of job, then you might want to develop a separate job objective for each resume. For now, if you are going to look for only one kind of job, or if you will be applying for positions just like the one you have now, you should complete this section. If you will be looking for jobs that go by a variety of titles, skip this section altogether.

THE JOB OBJECTIVE WORKSHEET

Use the space provided on the Job Objective Worksheet to put your job objective into words. Try beginning with a phrase like this: "Seeking a position as..." or "Looking for a job in...." Be as specific as possible. If you find that you sound vague or general, abandon your efforts and be content with your "Qualifications Summary." For example, "Seeking a position as administrative assistant" is a good place to start if you know the title of the job you will be looking for. If you're not quite sure of the title, but you know the job field, you might consider an objective like "Looking for an entry-level job in advertising."

For a little more impact, you can add information about yourself. Try stealing a phrase or two from your "Qualifications Summary." For example: "Experienced administrative assistant, with three years of progressively responsible experience, seeks position where knowledge and skills can be applied." (Notice how this emphasizes experience, includes a number, and conveys the idea of serving an employer.) The inexperienced job seeker might try something like "Creative, hard-working young person seeks entry-level position in advertising."

MAKE A CONTRIBUTION

Remember that your job objective must make you look like the kind of employee who can make a contribution to a company or organization. The most common mistake made in writing job objectives is to focus on your own needs instead of focusing on the needs of your employer-to-be. Typical examples of this kind of mistake include phrases like these: "Seeking rewarding position..."; "Looking for a position that offers rapid advancement..."; "Seeking a job that allows relocation to Sunbelt region..."; "Looking for a position that promises financial compensation commensurate with my experience...," etc.

The emphasis in the statements above is all on the employee, not the employer. Frankly, the only people who care about the needs of the job seeker are the job seeker and the job seeker's family. If you can't write a job objective that makes you look immediately like the kind of worker someone would want to hire, stick with the "Qualifications Summary" and forget the "Job Objective."

Several of the sample resumes at the end of this book do include Job Objectives. You might want to look through the samples before you try to write your own.

JOB OBJECTIVE WORKSHEET

You may not get your job objective worded perfectly on your first try, or even on your second try. There is space below to try three times. An additional worksheet is available too—either to develop more job objectives for additional resumes or to keep rewriting your first one until it sounds perfect to you. Skim through the sample resumes at the back of the book for examples and inspiration.

JOB OBJECTIVE (First draft)

_____
_____
_____
_____
_____

JOB OBJECTIVE (Second draft)

_____
_____
_____
_____
_____

JOB OBJECTIVE (Final version)

_____
_____
_____
_____
_____

Questions to ask in evaluating your "job objective."

—Will my objective immediately position me as a qualified candidate for the positions I am seeking?

—Does it emphasize the contribution I can make to a company or organization?

—Will it interest an employer in reading further down the page?

JOB OBJECTIVE WORKSHEET

You may not get your job objective worded perfectly on your first try, or even on your second try. There is space below to try three times. Use this additional worksheet to develop more job objectives for additional resumes or to keep rewriting your first one until it sounds perfect to you. Feel free to skim through the sample resumes at the back of the book for examples and inspiration.

JOB OBJECTIVE (First draft)

_____

_____

_____

_____

_____

JOB OBJECTIVE (Second draft)

_____

_____

_____

_____

_____

JOB OBJECTIVE (Final version)

_____

_____

_____

_____

_____

Questions to ask in evaluating your "job objective."

—Will my objective immediately position me as a qualified candidate for the positions I am seeking?

—Does it emphasize the contribution I can make to a company or organization?

—Will it interest an employer in reading further down the page?

14 ASSEMBLING YOUR RESUME

PUTTING IT ALL TOGETHER!

Good news! Now that you have created each of the components of your resume, all you have to do is assemble them and your resume will be complete! Since you have all of the pieces, you can assemble your resume in exactly the way you choose. This approach allows you to create one resume to use throughout your job search or to design a "customized" resume every time you need a resume.

You probably have a specific job in your mind right now. If you don't have a job in mind, you probably know the type of work you will be looking for. Think about your job goals as you put together your resume.

You don't have to use everything you have written so far. There may be items on your worksheets that you want to leave off your resume altogether. There may be entire worksheets that you don't want to include. These are your decisions.

There are very few strict rules to follow in creating a resume. There is not one "right way" to do it. Everything that follows is good advice, but it is not rigid. Remember that your objective is to design a resume that will get you an interview. Nobody knows your strengths and capabilities better than you do. Here is your opportunity to tell your next employer exactly what you can contribute. Hold that thought, and let's get started putting your resume together.

HEADING

Start your resume with your name, address, and phone number at the top of the page. Since prospective employers are likely to call during the day, try to provide a phone number where you can be reached during regular business hours. If that is not possible for you, use a number where a message can be left for you. (You may want to consider purchasing or borrowing an answering machine, contracting with an answering service for the duration of your job search, or securing an electronic "mail box" from your local phone company.) If you simply cannot be contacted during normal working hours, note next to your phone number the hours that are best to reach you. (Take a look at the sample resumes to see how others handle this.) If you have a fax number that prospective employers can use to contact you, include this under your phone number.

NOTE: It is not necessary to label your resume with the word "Resume." The people who receive your resume will know what it is.

JOB OBJECTIVE

As we discussed in the section on writing a job objective, it is not necessary to have an objective on your resume. Only when your job objective matches the position you are applying for does the job objective really "work." The problem with having an objective that doesn't correspond directly with your target job is that it looks as if you prepared your resume with a different job in mind. This may raise concerns in the mind of your prospective employer from the start.

If you are planning to look for work in only one field and you have prepared a job objective that is relevant to that field, feel free to use it at the beginning of your resume. If you are able to prepare a new resume each time you apply for a new job, you can modify your job objective so that it exactly matches the job. Otherwise, you might consider a "Qualifications Summary" instead (you have already prepared this on an earlier worksheet).

There isn't much point in vague job objectives like "Seeking a position that utilizes my talents" or "Want a challenging position in which I can apply my skills." Remember that employers want to know what you can do for them. Your personal goals aren't all that important here. Avoid saying what you hope to get from a job and focus on what you have to contribute!

QUALIFICATIONS SUMMARY

After you completed your skills, personal qualifications, "work experience," accomplishments, and job skills worksheets, you compiled a summary of your qualifications—the qualities that make you an asset to an employer. You might begin your resume with this "Qualifications Summary." Look back at it now and evaluate it as a way to start off your resume. Does it communicate to a potential employer your skills, personal qualifications, or experience in a way that makes you look like a person who could make a contribution to an employer? If the answer is "yes," consider starting your resume with this statement. You could call it "Qualifications" or "Summary," or you could make up your own category. You might also include it with no heading at all. Because it is at the top of your resume, it will be seen (and read) by everyone. It is the perfect place to "introduce" yourself to a possible employer.

YOUR GREATEST ASSETS

After you have stated your job objective or provided a summary of your qualifications, it's time to put forth your strongest qualifications for the jobs you want. These will be different for each resume writer. Fortunately, all you have to do is choose from what you have already written. Look back over your skills worksheets, your personal qualifications worksheets, your accomplishments worksheets, your experience worksheets, and your education worksheets. Which one set is likely to be most important to your prospective employers?

Traditionally, resume writers have concentrated on their experiences, but this has not always served them well. If your experience isn't very extensive, or isn't very impressive, why give it such a prominent position in your resume? Your skills, qualifications, or accomplishments might give your resume a much better start. It is often better to begin with one of these anyway, since employers will always continue to read down your resume until they find your experience and your education. Knowing that, you can save these two categories until the end of your resume if they are not your greatest assets.

Here are some guidelines to follow. Keep in mind that these are only suggestions. Your goal is to present your qualifications in the order you think is right for you. You get to decide how you are going to present yourself on paper to possible employers.

Guidelines for Great Assets

1. Experience: If you are looking for a job that is closely related to previous jobs you have held, consider putting your experience first.

2. Accomplishments: If you have some impressive accomplishments to your credit (whether they are work-related or not), you might want to list these first, just to get the reader's attention. If they arouse curiosity about you, they will keep the reader reading.

3. Education: If you have recently graduated from college or have recently acquired a degree, diploma, or certificate that is directly related to the work you are seeking, think about stating that right at the beginning. This is especially true if you don't feel that you have impressive skills, qualifications, accomplishments, or experience.

If you are presently enrolled in an educational program that is directly related to the job you are hoping to obtain, you can treat this just as if you already had a certificate or degree. Just note that you are "presently enrolled" and then list the type of program, the subjects or courses, honors or awards, and other information that is relevant to an employer. If you are attending school while you are working (even if you are taking courses without formal enrollment in a program), include that fact on your resume.

If you do put your education first, try to include a mention of particularly important classes, your grade point average (if it is higher than a "B"), your class rank (if it is in the top 20% or so), and other facts that highlight your educational achievements. See the sample resumes for examples of how others have handled this.

4. Skills: If you have a skills list that is especially appealing to a prospective employer (and you probably do), it is always a good way to begin. You want your skills list to arouse enough interest to keep a prospective employer reading your resume. Most lists draw a reaction something like this: "These skills look like ones we could use." If yours can get a similar response, put your skills list first.

5. Personal qualifications: Even if you don't think that you have a great deal to offer, you do have your personal qualifications. These are definitely an asset; they are uniquely yours; and they are a fine place to start a resume. Maybe you are looking for your first job; maybe you are returning to work after a long absence; or maybe you are changing careers to an area in which you have no previous experience. Your personal qualifications may be the perfect place to begin.

As you will see on the sample resumes, you don't have to call your personal assets "personal qualifications." You can title this section "Profile," or "Strengths," or "Skills," or "Expertise"—or you can make up any other heading you like.

The point is to draw attention to your strengths as a candidate, whatever they may be.

MORE ASSETS

Once you have selected the section that you think presents you most favorably to a possible employer, you can let the other sections fall into place below that one. Look over your worksheets for experience, skills, qualifications, accomplishments, and education. Decide whether there are any you want to leave out altogether, and then put the rest into the order that best presents your strengths. Remember that employers are likely to keep reading until they find your experience and your education, so put those after your skills, qualifications, and accomplishments, unless they are more important than the other possible sections.

AWARDS, MEMBERSHIPS, PUBLICATIONS

After you have included all of the information listed under "More Assets" above, it's time to take a look at the rest of your worksheets and put them into the order of their importance. If you have completed these worksheets, take a look at them now and decide how you would like to order them in your resume. You don't have to include them at all, but try to work them into this first draft. You can see how you like them later.

PERSONAL INFORMATION

Including any personal information on your resume is entirely optional. You are not obligated to include this information. However, if you feel that it is a boost to your candidacy for a position, this is the place to include it.

REFERENCES

Look back at the references worksheet you prepared. If you want to include your references—the names, titles, addresses, and phone numbers of people who can tell potential employers about you—they should go at the end of your resume. If you are not planning to put names in your resume, you can either leave the "references" section out altogether or you can include a line that says "References available on request."

CONFIDENTIALITY

There are many reasons that job-seekers may want their resumes kept confidential. The most obvious reason, of course, is that they don't want a present employer to know that they are looking for another job. If you ask that your application for a position (or even your inquiry about the availability of a position) be kept confidential, your request will usually be honored. If you do want your resume to be considered a confidential document, you should state that on the resume itself.

Although you can put a note at the top of the first page of your resume that states "CONFIDENTIAL RESUME," it is more common to include a note at the end of your resume. It can have a heading of its own (like "Education" or "References"), but it doesn't have to be this prominent. A clear note at the bottom of your resume can be sufficient. It might state: "This resume is submitted in confidence. Please keep confidential." It can address a specific concern: "Please do not contact present employer." Or it can be a simple declaration: "Please respect the confidentiality of this resume."

15 PRINTING YOUR RESUME

HOW TO GET THE BEST RESULTS

The appearance of your resume is important. Because your resume will usually be compared with many others, it needs to be competitive. This doesn't mean that you must use dramatic graphics or arresting typefaces, but it does mean that you need to pay attention to what your resume looks like. You have put a lot of time and energy into the words that make up your resume, and it is worth putting a little more time and attention into its appearance.

WORD PROCESSING

Whatever appearance you have in mind for your resume, your first step is to have it typed on a word processor. You can do this directly from the worksheets you have prepared in earlier sections of this book or you can write out a version by hand that puts everything in exactly the order you want. If you have access to a word processor, and you are a decent typist, you can enter all of your information yourself. If you aren't able to use a word processor, you might know someone who can help you out. If you don't have a friend—or a friend of a friend—who can enter your resume into a word processor, you can turn to a typing, word processing, or secretarial service in your community. You can find this kind of help in your local telephone directory.

It might take a couple of tries to get everything to look just right and to fit properly. You will probably have to do some editing to get the material from your worksheets into the format you want. You will also need to do some proofreading to check for spelling mistakes. Most word processing systems have built-in "spelling checkers" that can check the spelling once the resume has been typed, but you will still need to check the overall accuracy. If you are not a good speller or proofreader, get some help from someone who is. If you have used a professional service, it should be able to provide help with this checking.

All of the entering of information into the word processor is known as "inputting." You are putting information in. The next stage is the "outputting," or printing. Whether you do the typing yourself or have someone do it for you, you will do your proofreading on the "output"—a printed piece of paper (also known in computer-speak as "hard copy"). The printer may be able to produce a very professional-looking printed copy, or it may only be able to turn out a copy that is decent enough for proofreading but not good enough to actually call your resume.

Some printers that are hooked up to word processors are able to produce different typefaces, and in different sizes as well. You or your typist can manipulate the appearance of the type on the page to get just the look you want. You will find a variety of resumes in the sample pages that follow. You might want to choose one or more that really appeal to you so that you can use them as models when you prepare your own. If you or your typist can produce a printed copy that satisfies you, you can skip the next paragraph and go directly to the section below entitled "Printing vs. Photocopying."

If you do not have access to a printer that can give you the kind of printed version you want, you still have options available. If you can get a diskette (a "floppy disk") from the word processor, you should be able to take it to a business in your community that has the kind of printer you need to produce the resume you want. Again, you might take samples from this book to show to the person who will be formatting the output to get the results you are looking for. If you don't know where to turn for a high-quality printout of your resume, check your local telephone directory under headings like "typesetting," "desktop publishing," or "printing." Often these same businesses can help you get your resume printed or copied as well (see below).

PRINTING VS. PHOTOCOPYING

Once you have one copy of your completed resume, you can have additional copies printed or photocopied. Photocopying is cheaper and faster and can often produce excellent copies. Professional printing will always produce outstanding copies (if your original is outstanding), but it may not be worth the extra expense to you.

Generally, if you are planning to have fewer than 100 copies made, you should turn to a photocopying service that uses high-speed, high-quality copy machines. Photocopies cost only a few cents apiece and should look nearly as good as your original. Copy services offer a choice of papers, sometimes with matching envelopes (see the next section for more information on paper selection), and they can often do the copying while you wait. You can also ask to see what a copy will look like on different papers and—for a very small charge—the copy service will run these for you so that you can decide which you like best. If you are not sure where you can find a copy service, check your local telephone directory under such headings as "photocopying" or "copying and duplicating services."

If you are planning to have more than 100 copies made, you can still use a photocopying service, but you might also investigate offset printing as well. There are at least three reasons to consider using a printing service instead of a copying service:

1) You have designed a resume that will be difficult to reproduce well on a photocopier, because of the typefaces you have selected or the surface texture of the paper you want to use (photocopying works better on smooth papers than on textured papers);

2) You work in a field that values appearances highly (graphic arts, fine arts, or any design-related field, for example);

3) You are seeking a high-level position (middle manager or above), in which other applicants are likely to have well-designed and printed resumes.

Fortunately, printers frequently offer a range of printing services and can usually advise you on the type of printing that will best meet your needs. Take your original with you to a commercial printer, tell the printer how many copies you need and the kind of paper you want to use, and ask for advice. In one shop these days you may find both copying and printing services. If you don't know of a printing service in your community, check your telephone directory under such headings as "printers" or "copying and duplicating services."

PAPER SELECTION

The paper you select for your resume is not vital to the success of the resume. Resumes that are cleanly printed on plain white paper and meet all of the criteria outlined on the "Resume Checklist" (see page 92) can be just as well received by potential employers as those that are printed on colored and textured paper and arrive in matching envelopes, with cover letters computer-printed on matching paper. However, it is true that employers receive many resumes, especially for advertised positions. Even though they try to select candidates to interview based on what is on the paper (and not the paper itself), it is hard not to be influenced by appearances. This is especially true in businesses where appearances are an important part of the work, such as design and art-related enterprises, architecture, interior decorating, and similar ventures.

Generally speaking, it costs very little more money to have your resume copied or printed onto colored paper than onto white paper. Some copy services and printers stock envelopes to match selected papers, and all will be happy to sell you extra sheets of the paper you select for your resume so that you can use matching paper for your cover letters. Ask to see available papers and ask directly about the comparative costs before you make your selection.

KEEP COLOR CONSERVATIVE

As far as color is concerned, keep it conservative unless you know that you will be looking for work in a job field that values creativity. In most fields it is fine to stand out a little in a pile of resumes, but it is not OK to stand out a lot. Off-white paper colors and so-called "neutrals" are safe choices if you want to move away from white. These may have names like "cream," "tan," "buff," "ivory," etc. Very pale shades of blue or gray are also fine. If you are in doubt about a color, stay with a light one.

There are several other reasons to stay with a light-colored paper that has very little texture to it (in other words, a "smooth-finish" paper). First, it is likely that your resume will be photocopied after it is received by a prospective employer, and light colors photocopy better than dark colors.

The second reason to keep the paper color light (and the ink dark) is the likelihood that you or an employer will fax your resume and you will want the fax to transmit as cleanly as possible.

A third reason to keep the paper light and smooth is the growing use of "scanners." These machines optically "scan" your resume to put it into a computerized database.Once scanned, a resume can be assigned to various headings under which it can be "filed" and transmitted electronically to selected employees throughout the corporation (and around the world). Like copiers and fax machines, scanners produce their best results when there is the greatest contrast between paper and ink.

ENVELOPE SELECTION

For your cover letters, it is a nice touch—but certainly not necessary—to use paper that matches the paper of your resume. You can purchase extra sheets inexpensively when you have your resume printed and you can type your cover letters directly on these sheets (or put the sheets into the printer for your word processor). Again, this is not essential. It is just another way to make you look attractive as a job candidate, and you should take advantage of the opportunity if you can.

It is not essential that you have matching envelopes (since your envelope is likely to be tossed out as soon as it is opened), so this is one place where you can save some money. You also don't need to have envelopes printed with your name and address. This is expensive and not usually necessary (unless you are looking for a very high-level job). However, it is important that your envelopes be typed and not handwritten if this is possible for you to do.

One investment that is worth considering (and it is a small additional expense) is the purchase of envelopes that are larger than standard business envelopes. The standard envelope requires you to fold your resume and cover letter twice to fit it into the envelope. A larger, 5" x 7" envelope requires only one fold, and the still-larger 9" x 12" envelope allows you to insert both cover letter and resume without a fold at all.

The larger sizes also make your resume stand out in the mail and may help your envelope be opened before others. But it is the fold lines that are the most important reason to think about using a large envelope. As discussed in the section on paper selection, there is a good chance that your resume will be photocopied, faxed, or scanned after it is received by an employer. All of these processes work better when the "original" is a flat, unfolded piece of paper. The extra effort you make to ensure that your resume (and cover letter) arrive in great condition may pay off for you in ways that you can only anticipate now. It's worth a thought on your part.

CUSTOMIZED RESUMES

Just as cover letters need to be individualized every time you send out your resume, it can be argued that your resume is most effective if it is customized to each job you apply for. Because every job has slightly different requirements, you might emphasize slightly different experiences or qualifications every time you apply for a position. If you have easy access to a word processor and are pretty good at using it—or you have a friend or colleague who can do the work for you at a reasonable cost—you might consider reshaping your resume every time you apply for a job.

Customizing your resume is not as difficult (or as wacky) as it might sound. When you know the requirements for a particular position you simply evaluate your resume, and the worksheets you used to prepare it, to see if you have presented yourself as a truly qualified candidate. Sometimes you will want to reorder your qualifications. Other times you may choose to expand the description of a particular experience that is especially relevant. The word processor allows you to move text around quickly, and the worksheets you completed earlier in this book give you the additional material you might want to use.

To print your customized resume, you can "output" directly from the word processor's printer onto nearly any paper you choose or you can go through any of the steps outlined above to produce a printed version. Obviously this approach makes the most sense when you have access to a printer that is able to produce a product you feel is ready to send. With this capability you can easily produce individualized resumes as well as individualized cover letters—and print both on the same paper as well.

If you are planning to look for work in more than one career field, you will probably need more than one version of your resume. It is common for job seekers to have a different version for each type of job they are seeking. Even if you choose not to customize your resume, you will want to have different resumes for different types of positions. For example, if you are planning to apply for jobs in sales and in marketing, you may want to consider having two resumes—one that emphasizes your qualifications and experiences in sales and one that highlights your qualifications and experiences in marketing. You can have these photocopied or printed, and you can even have them put onto the same type of paper if you want to. Just remember which is which and use the resumes accordingly.

16 COVER LETTERS

BUILDING BRIDGES BETWEEN RESUMES AND JOBS

The cover letter is the letter that you will send to prospective employers along with your resume. It has a very clear purpose: the cover letter links your resume to the position you are seeking. It is a bridge that you construct between yourself and your employer-to-be. Whether you are applying for a specific job that is currently available or are simply asking what might be available, you will need a cover letter. In fact, your resume should never be put into the mail without a cover letter. Fortunately, a good cover letter is easy to prepare.

The key point to keep in mind when you write a cover letter is what you have to contribute to an employer. The most common mistake that job-seekers make in developing their cover letters is to focus on their own needs—the reasons that they are applying for positions. What employers want to know is what you can do for them—not what they can do for you. So, to write a successful cover letter, you have to think like an employer.

It might help you in writing your cover letters to picture yourself sitting at a desk opening one envelope after another, each one holding a resume and a cover letter. If you're like most employers, you will be making three piles out of these resumes and cover letters: YES (I think I'll call the person behind this resume and schedule an interview); MAYBE (the person I see described on paper looks kind of interesting, but not as interesting as the people in the YES pile); and NO (this candidate just doesn't look qualified). Your challenge is to get your cover letter and resume into the YES pile. A good cover letter can make the difference between the MAYBE pile and the YES pile. Since most employers never get beyond the YES stack, your cover letter has a vital part to play in your job search.

A COVER LETTER FOR EVERY RESUME

Not only do you have to send a cover letter with every resume you put into the mail, but you have to send a different letter with every resume. At the very least, you will change the address of your prospective employer and the title of the job you are applying for. When you are looking for only one kind of position, these small changes may be the only modifications you will need to make to your cover letter. However, if you are seeking different kinds of jobs, you will definitely need different types of cover letters.

This is not quite as intimidating as it sounds. As you will see below, cover letters are not very long and they are not very difficult to write. Avoid the temptation to say the same thing in every letter you write (and definitely avoid the temptation to have one letter printed or copied to accompany every resume you send). The extra time you spend on your cover letter can make the difference between getting called for an interview and being forgotten. If you are going to write, take the time to do it right.

WRITING THE COVER LETTER

There are only a few critical ingredients in a cover letter. Let's look at them in the order in which they will appear on paper.

Date

Write down the date and now you're on your way! (It's such a painless way to get started.)

Employer and address

Whenever possible, direct your letter and resume to a specific person, and include that person's title as well. If you don't know who the correct person is, pick up the telephone and call. If you don't do it now, you will kick yourself later when you want to follow up with another letter or call. Similarly, if you are not sure of the spelling of a name or the exact title of the person, call and find out. You will hurt your chances if you don't. (Nobody likes to have a name misspelled or a title misstated.) Obviously, you need to make sure that you have the address correct as well.

Salutation

If you know the gender of the person you are addressing, a simple "Dear Ms. _____" or "Dear Mr. _____" is fine. If you don't know the gender, call and ask (you won't be the only person who has ever inquired). If you really can't find out, write out the person's full name after the word "Dear." If you do not have a name in the address, simply skip the salutation altogether. (The days of writing "To whom it may concern" or "Dear sir or madam" are long gone.)

First paragraph: WHY

The first paragraph has one purpose: to state exactly WHY you are writing. Are you applying for a position that was advertised? If so, where was it advertised? Are you writing without knowing about an opening? If so, why did you pick this person or organization?

The first paragraph can be very brief, as you will see in the sample cover letters that follow.

Second paragraph: WHAT

In the second paragraph, you describe WHAT you have to offer to this particular employer. You can make general remarks about yourself, but try to back them up with specific examples if you can. This paragraph will probably change from one letter to another, although you may come up with phrases that you can use in more than one cover letter. For some letters, you might want to emphasize your experience, if it is directly relevant to a position you are seeking. In another, you may want to highlight your personal qualities, if they seem to match the requirements of the job. For still another letter, you could note your education, including individual courses you took that prepared you for the job you hope to secure. This is the spot where you build the "bridge" between your qualifications and the needs of the employer.

This paragraph is the heart of your cover letter. It shows the employer that you have thought about the job (or the organization) and believe that you can make a genuine contribution. (If you don't think that you can make a genuine contribution you probably shouldn't waste your time—and the employer's—by writing.) This is your chance to feature one or two specifics from your past that might positively impress a prospective employer. Have you taken on a project that demonstrates your initiative? Have you solved a problem in a way that saved time or money for a previous employer or organization? Have you faced challenges that are similar to those you are likely to face in this new position?

Feel free to "raid" your resume for examples and phrases. You can take any material in your resume and use it directly in your cover letter if it supports the point you want to make. You have already put a lot of effort into developing the wording of your resume and you do not have to reword it now if it works "as is." If it suits your purposes, use it. If not, rework it until it does. For example, you might want to add more detail about an accomplishment or a previous job in your cover letter than you included on your resume because the experience relates directly to the position you are applying for. One or two examples are all you need.

Remember: this is the place where you establish your qualifications. You want to "hook" the reader into reading your resume to find out more about you. Don't try to condense your whole resume into a one-paragraph summary. This part of the cover letter is just a "taste" of what is on the resume. Your challenge here is to make the reader want to find out more about you.

Third paragraph: HOW

This is your final paragraph. You want to let the reader know HOW to reach you to set up an interview. (Do you want to be called at work or at home? What are the best times to call?) You also want to state HOW you are going to proceed. (Are you going to call to follow up? If so, when?) Finally, you should state HOW you have responded to any specific requests the employer has made. (Were you asked to submit a sample of your previous work? A list of references?) Use this paragraph to address these requests.

Closing

Close your letter as you would any business letter. Use a businesslike closing word or phrase and follow it with your signature, your address, and your phone number(s). If you are using letterhead stationery that includes the address and phone number you want to use for contacts with prospective employers, you don't need to repeat the information in your closing.

You will find several different closing words on the sample cover letters that follow. Choose one that you like. Don't get too cute (don't use phrases like "Expectantly yours," for example). Remember that this is a business transaction and you will do fine.

A special note on "Salary History"

There is one request that is frequently made by employers in advertised openings that you DON'T have to address directly in your cover letters. This is the request for your "salary requirements" or for a "salary history." Unless you have very firm salary demands—so firm that you are willing to take yourself out of the running for a position even before you receive an interview—you should not name a precise dollar figure in your cover letter. Don't state exactly what you earn now and don't state what you expect your next job to pay.

Let's face it. There are many more factors to a job than salary alone. There may be a great benefits package to consider. Maybe the opportunities for advancement are tremendous. Or perhaps you're desperate for a job and would work for almost anything. Whatever your personal situation, the salary question is one that should be answered vaguely. It is perfectly acceptable to include a statement like "My salary requirements are flexible." You might follow that with "I will be happy to discuss them in an interview."

Even if you are sure that you know what the salary is when you are applying for a job, being vague in your cover letter can still pay off for you. Most jobs have salary ranges attached to them instead of one specific figure. You don't want to state an amount at the low end of the range because that is what you are likely to be offered if you get the job. At the same time, you don't want to give a figure at the high end of the range because you may be seen as greedy or out of the reach of the employer.

If you have a specific salary in mind, it is still best not to be too direct. For example, if you are making $34,000 per year now, you might say in your cover letter: "I expect that the position will offer a salary in the high 30's." Even if you know that the salary has a wide range, don't request a range yourself. (Don't write "I am looking for a job that pays in the mid to high 30's," because you are bound to be offered a salary at the low end of your own stated range.) Notice, too, in our example that the expectation was stated in terms of what the position might pay, not in terms of what the job seeker was demanding. Although employers believe that they want to hear the salary requirements of applicants, they often discriminate against candidates who directly state salary demands in their cover letters.

On the next page, you will find a checklist to use in evaluating your cover letter. Read it now, and then read it again after you have drafted a letter of your own. After the checklist there are several sample cover letters. None of these is exactly right for your situation, but you should be able to get direction and inspiration here for writing your own cover letters. Look these over and start writing.

COVER LETTER CHECKLIST

Use this checklist to critique your cover letters. If you can answer "yes" to every question, you have an excellent cover letter—and an excellent chance of getting an interview. If you can't answer "yes" to every question, go back and make a few changes to your letter.

1. Is your cover letter addressed to a specific person? (Are you sure that this is the correct person and that you have spelled the name and the title correctly?)

2. Does your letter state clearly why you are writing?

3. Does your letter tell the employer why you are qualified for the position you are seeking? Does it provide examples of your qualifications?

4. Does your letter tell an employer what you can contribute to the organization? Do you include accomplishments or personal qualifications that suggest the contributions you can make?

5. Does your letter highlight the most relevant facts about you and your background? Do you connect those facts directly to the needs of the employer?

6. Does your letter use "action words" to describe your accomplishments, skills, and qualifications?

7. Does your letter respond directly to an ad or job description? If so, does it address each of the points mentioned in the ad or description?

8. Does your letter avoid "jargon" that might not be understood by the recipient?

9. Is your letter persuasive? Does it encourage the reader to read the resume?

10. Does your letter avoid negative statements and apologies?

11. Have you cut out anything that seems vague or insincere?

12. Are the paragraphs short (no more than five lines each)?

13. Does your letter fit neatly onto one page?

14. Is your letter well typed and presented?

15. Does your letter include your name, address, and phone number?

January 10, 1994

Janet Schroeder, President
Schroeder Public Relations
119 Brattle Street
Cambridge, MA 02138

Dear Ms. Schroeder:

I am responding to your recent ad in the *Boston Globe*. I believe that I am well qualified for the position of Public Relations Associate and I know that I could make a significant contribution to your firm.

Although I have enclosed my resume, let me quickly highlight some of my relevant experiences. Through my in-depth internship at Morris-Bradshaw Public Relations, I had hands-on experience writing more than 25 press releases in less than four months. I followed through on all aspects of these releases, including their packaging and mailing. I have also written press releases for a local candidate for the Massachusetts state senate and conducted numerous phone surveys. I understand how a public relations firm works, I learn quickly, and I am comfortable working under deadlines.

I hope that we will be able to meet in person to discuss the Associate position. If I don't hear from you next week, I will give your secretary a call during the week of January 24th to see if I might make an appointment. I look forward to speaking with you soon.

Sincerely,

Helen Bueller

29 Oldbridge Road
Warwick, MA 01364

January 17, 1994

19 Westfield Avenue
Hartford, CT 06112

Ms. Joanne Ramirez, Principal
Oak Road Elementary School
1445 Oak Road Stratford, CT 06497

Dear Ms. Ramirez:

Nancy Brooks, a fourth grade teacher at Oak Road Elementary, has informed me that you have an opening for a second grade teacher for the school year that begins next September. I may be early in applying for the position but I believe I that I have a lot to offer to you and to your students.

I have enclosed my resume, which will present you with my background. What the resume cannot express is my enthusiasm for teaching children. Although I have only recently graduated from college, I have far more experience than most recent graduates. As you will see on my resume, I have taught third grade full-time, have substituted in every grade from kindergarten through sixth, and have volunteered as a Teacher's Aide for a year and a half. I am effective as a classroom teacher, tireless with children, and I can communicate well with fellow teachers and with parents.

I would like to have the opportunity to meet with you at your convenience. Although next fall seems like a long time from now, Nancy told me that you are hoping to fill the position by the end of February. I hope that I will hear from you by February 1. If I don't, I will give you a call to set up an appointment. I look forward to meeting you.

Sincerely,

Melinda Dalessio

January 24, 1994

James T. Chou
Software Applications Manager
Psy Tech, Inc.
11495 Lakeshore Drive
Minneapolis, MN 55429

Dear Mr. Chou:

I am writing to you because I believe that I could make a vital contribution to your division at Psy Tech. In my present position at Physical Systems, Inc., I have developed software that meets the requirements of physicists, hardware engineers, and systems programmers. I have served as the primary systems representative in the physical sciences lab. Since Psy Tech is in the same industry, I am sure that you have similar needs in your division.

I have enclosed my resume, which will provide you with additional information on my experience. You will see that I regularly troubleshoot both hardware and software problems and train end users in software applications.

I know that you may not have openings in your division at the present time, but I think that it would be mutually beneficial for us to meet, whether or not there are positions available. It is always worthwhile to know more about the competition. Although our companies are not in direct competition, I think it could pay to get together. I will give you a call on February 1st to see when we can schedule an appointment. Feel free to call me before then if it is more convenient for you. My work number is (218) 972-1342.

Thank you in advance for your time and consideration.

Sincerely,

Orlando Titus

October 10, 1993

Hollis Horsten
Personnel Manager
Vacutron, Inc.
11929 Beach Road
Honolulu, HI 96810

I am writing at the suggestion of Bruce Schwab, who works in your Quality Control Department. Bruce thinks that my skills in organizing and supervising would be an asset at Vacutron.

At present I am an Assistant Air Department Officer at the Naval Air Warfare Center in Honolulu. I expect to receive my honorable discharge from the Navy at the end of December. My experiences in the armed forces are directly relevant to your needs at Vacutron. As you will see on my resume, much of my military career has involved administration of large-scale operations. Currently I supervise 25 air traffic controllers, 15 equipment maintenance technicians, and 10 aircraft line handlers. In less than five years I have contributed to reducing the cost of aircraft maintenance by 25% and have overseen a reduction in staffing of 35%. I have personally supervised the transition of my department to a new computer system, running two systems in parallel for six months.

I think that these are exactly the kinds of skills that Vacutron could use. I would like the opportunity to discuss with you the ways in which I can make a contribution to the company. Please look over the resume that I have enclosed and give me a call. If I haven't heard from you by the end of next week, I will call you to set up an appointment. Even if you don't have a specific position in mind, or an immediate job opening, I think that our getting together will be worth your time. I look forward to speaking with you soon.

Sincerely,

Kent Zelinka

2903-B Kuaui Road
Honolulu, HI 96816
(808) 982-2873

17 RESUME TIPS

WHAT TO DO AND WHAT NOT TO DO

DO!

1. "Hook" your readers. Near the top of your resume, include some key points about yourself that will make the reader want to find out more about you. A summary of your accomplishments, experience, personal qualities, or skills is an excellent way to do this.

2. Highlight your strengths. You probably know the saying "If you've got it, flaunt it." This is certainly true on your resume. Your prospective employer should be able to see quickly what you have to offer. Again, a concise summary of your best "selling points" at the top of the resume can communicate your strengths at a glance.

3. Structure your resume like a pyramid. The most important things about you should be near the top. There is no formula that you have to follow in assembling the component parts of your resume, but you should start with your best features. Remember that most employers will continue to read (if they like what they see) until they reach your experience and education. Since you know that, you can put important facts about yourself (in order of their importance) between your name at the top and your experience or education.

4. Be sure your resume is easy to read. If your resume is jammed with words, difficult to follow, or badly laid out on the page, no one is going to take the time to read it—even if you are a great job candidate. If you can't judge for yourself, ask a friend to evaluate your resume for you. Also, take a look at the sample resumes at the end of this book for inspiration.

5. **Keep your sentences short**. Start as many as you can with "action words" (a list of these is provided for you). It's OK to drop words like "a," "an," and "the."

6. **Help your readers know what to read**. Use "bullets," dashes or other typographic devices to assist prospective employers in focusing on your strengths. Use plenty of "white space" between points to make each point stand out.

7. **Support your objective**. If you have a job objective, be sure that your resume shows clearly why you are qualified for the job you are seeking. Information that doesn't relate to your job objective should be reworded so that it does relate or it should be dropped altogether.

8. **Keep your resume to one or two pages**. Most employers don't want to read more than two pages. They will read more if you are an incredibly experienced person with terrific credentials, but you're safer staying at no more than two pages.

9. **If your resume is two pages, say so on page one**. All you need to type is one line, like "Continued on next page." You can also print on the back of the first page, but be sure to include something like "See reverse side" or simply "Turn over."

10. **Answer the question that every employer asks**. Your resume must address the question that is in the employer's mind: "What can this person do for me?" If your resume can answer that question, you can get an interview—and an interview can land you a job. One of the best ways to answer the question is to include summaries of your personal qualities, experience, skills, and accomplishments.

DON'T!

1. **Don't lie**. You can never make a lie work in your favor. Don't stretch the truth too far either—it will break!

2. **Don't copy someone else's resume**. You are unique and your resume needs to reflect your uniqueness. You can take inspiration from other resumes, including the samples in this book, and you can borrow elements from the resumes of others, but make your resume your own.

3. **Don't write long sentences**. Remember that your resume will be read quickly and set it up so that it can be read easily.

4. Don't use long lines. Lines that run all the way across a page take too long to read and make it easy for readers to lose interest. Just as you must keep your sentences short, you must keep your lines short too.

5. Don't put more than four lines together in one "block." Employers need to be able to read at a glance. If you have more than four short lines, you are probably trying to say too much. Divide a long block of text into two points.

6. Don't be vague. Be as specific as possible. Include facts and figures wherever you can. If you are vague, be sure that you are vague on purpose (for example, you might choose to say "Service position in food service industry" instead of "Waitress in a coffee shop").

7. Don't include information that is not relevant to an employer. Select from your experience, accomplishments, personal qualities, and skills those that relate most closely to the job you hope to obtain. There is a good rule to follow in evaluating whether or not something is relevant: "If in doubt, leave it out."

8. Don't include "personal" information. There is almost never a need to include such data as your height, weight, age, marital status, number of children, etc. This kind of information hasn't been included in resumes for more than twenty years and most employers would be shocked and dismayed to see it.

9. Don't list a reference unless you have the person's permission. Of course, it's important too to know that you will get a positive recommendation!

10. Don't build your resume around dates. Dates should be put at the end of any description—not at the beginning—or they should be left out altogether. When you did anything is not as important as what you did. If you emphasize dates, you give the reader the opportunity to play "The Dating Game": "Let's see how all these dates fit together"; "Maybe there's a gap in here and I'll find it"; etc. Don't provide the opportunity. Don't let dates stand out!

THE RESUME CHECKLIST 18

EVALUATING YOUR RESUME

Here is one way to evaluate the resume you have written. If you can answer "Yes" to all of the following questions, then you have a resume that should work well for you in your job search (or in your efforts to move up in the organization you work for now). This is not the only way to "critique" your resume. You should have other people give you feedback as well: colleagues, friends, family, and (most importantly) people who are already employed in the type of job that you are seeking. Remember, though, that many people have misguided and out-of-date ideas about what a resume should look like, so you will have to ignore some of the "advice" you receive.

If you can't answer "Yes" to all of the questions here, try to see what is standing between your resume and "Yes." What can you modify on your resume so that your answer is an unqualified "Yes"? It is probably worth the time and effort it will take to make those changes. If you need motivation, remember that there is probably someone else looking for the same jobs that you are who can answer "Yes" to all of these questions!

1. Does your resume present you as a well-qualified job candidate?

2. Does it convey your strongest "selling points" to a prospective employer?

3. Is it easy to read?

4. Does it invite reading through good design and professional appearance?

5. Are your greatest strengths closest to the top of your resume?

6. Are dates out of the "sight line" (at the end of descriptions, on the right side; not at the beginning of descriptions, on the left side)?

7. Does each description begin with an "action word"?

8. Are your sentences short, with no wasted words?

9. Have you used symbols (like dots, "bullets," dashes, etc.) to separate one point from another?

10. If you have an "objective" at the top of your resume, does the resume itself demonstrate how you are qualified for the position you're seeking?

11. Are you prepared to discuss everything on your resume with a potential employer?

12. Have you eliminated information that could be used to discriminate against you?

13. Is everything spelled correctly?

14. Is everything grammatically correct?

15. Are your name, address, and phone number(s) easy to find and read?

If you can answer "Yes" to the questions above, you are ready to use your resume as one of the most important parts of your job-seeking campaign. There are more tips and suggestions on the pages that follow.

SPECIAL TIPS 19

SUGGESTIONS FOR SPECIAL SITUATIONS

Nearly everyone who is writing a resume has a "special situation" that requires a special strategy or approach. This chapter suggests strategies and approaches for a number of the most frequently encountered special situations. You might want to skim through this chapter to see if you fall into any of these groups.

1. INEXPERIENCED OR LOOKING FOR A FIRST JOB

If you lack experience, build your resume around your other "selling points." You might even want to leave out altogether a section entitled "Experience." Read (and reread) the chapter on "Strategic Marketing." Then figure out what about you will be most appealing to the employers you plan to contact. Concentrate on communicating your skills, personal qualifications, accomplishments (no matter where you achieved them), and education. (See the sample resumes on pages 125, 128, 142, 144, and 148.)

2. STUDENT

If you are presently in school and looking for a full-time job (either right now or after graduation), you will not be expected to have a lot of relevant work experience. Instead, you will probably focus your resume on school-related activities. Although "Education" could be the first section on your resume, it is often advisable to start with a description of your personal qualities (which are called "Personal Qualifications" in this book and should be included on your resume that way too). This can help to bring you to life for an employer, most of whom are not too good at translating your student activities into job qualifications.

Your main task is to show how your courses, paid or volunteer work, and outside activities have prepared you for a full-time job. You should read the chapter entitled "Strategic Marketing" and complete all of the worksheets you can in this book. If you have leadership experience in any activity, highlight it. If you have good grades, be sure to note that on your resume. If you have managed to work, full-time or part-time, at ANY job while you have been in school, emphasize that fact (including the average number of hours per week you worked). You don't have to try to turn your part-time job as night custodian into more than it is. It is not so much the job that counts here as the fact that it shows responsibility and the ability to plan your time. (See resumes on pages 109, 111, 135, and 144.)

3. REENTERING THE WORK FORCE

If you have been out of the work force for a year or more, you probably have questions about how to explain your absence. You can leave out dates altogether on your resume and be prepared to answer questions if they come up in an interview; or you can explain the absence straightforwardly on your resume ("Recovering from injuries sustained in automobile accident, July 1993 to December 1993"). Employers often become wrapped up in their attempts to put together an exact chronology of your life from your resume. One way to discourage that is to emphasize your skills, personal qualifications, and accomplishments—and provide only a list of employers and positions held, without any dates at all. (See resumes on pages 140 and 145.)

4. SEEKING PART-TIME WORK OR FLEXIBLE HOURS

The place to discuss your interest in work that is not full-time is in your cover letter, not in your resume. In fact, you should not make any distinctions on your resume. Write your resume with the help of the worksheets in this book, just as if you were seeking a full-time job. Treat the opening of your cover letter the same way, stating the kind of work you are seeking and what you have to contribute. Once you have the employer's attention, you can bring up your interest in part-time or flexible hours. (See resumes on pages 140 and 145.)

5. CHANGING CAREERS

If you are trying to move from one career to another, you must create a resume and cover letter that demonstrate that you have the skills and personal qualifications that will allow you to do the job you are seeking. Employers can't be expected to make the connections between your previous experience and your desired job. You have to make the connections for them. This means that you have to understand the requirements of the job you are hoping to get and you must understand the needs of the employer (be sure to read the chapter on "Strategic Marketing"). (See resumes on pages 112 and 113.)

6. UNEMPLOYED

Like people reentering the workforce after an absence (see above), you do not have to include dates on your resume if you are unemployed. Removing dates makes employers focus on what you have to offer and not on when you worked where. This is not a "trick." It is an intelligent strategy. (And it is far better than listing your most recent job in an open-ended manner on your resume: "1992 to present," for example. This approach will only embarrass you if you are called in for an interview.) (See resumes on pages 120 and 127.)

Similarly, your cover letter can omit all mention of dates and can focus instead on your accomplishments, your experience, or the contributions you think you can make to the employer's organization.

7. FIRED OR LAID OFF

Although you will need to be prepared to discuss your firing or layoff in a job interview, you do not need to discuss it in your resume or cover letter. In preparing both, see the suggestions above under the headings "Unemployed" and "Reentering the Workforce." (See resumes on pages 121, 126, and 134.)

8. HANDICAPPED

The very term "handicapped" is being replaced by terms like "physically challenged" or "specially challenged." The new terms seem especially appropriate when discussing job-search strategies, including writing resumes and cover letters. It is against federal (and most state) laws to discriminate against people with handicapping conditions (unless the employer can prove that certain physical abilities are an essential part of a given job). Although attitudes are changing, partly as a result of this legislation and partly from the greater presence of people with disabilities in the work force, prejudice dies hard and prejudice against the "disabled" is still rampant.

If you are a physically challenged person, you can choose to mention that fact on your resume and in your cover letter or you can choose to ignore it. "Neglecting" to include your "disability" lets you compete directly with other candidates and reduces the chance that you will be a victim of an employer's bigotry or fear. However, you may have strong feelings about how you want to present yourself on paper. The decision is yours to make.

9. NEW CITIZEN OR NONCITIZEN

If much of your experience and many of your accomplishments have occurred outside the United States, prospective employers may be reluctant to interview and hire you for several reasons: they may not believe you know U.S. procedures and ways of doing business; they may worry about your language proficiency; and they may be concerned that the status of your citizenship will prove to be a problem for them.

Knowing these concerns in advance, you can address them in your resume and cover letter. At the bottom of your resume you might include a note entitled "Citizenship" or "Visa Status." In your descriptions of your experience, you might use U.S. terms wherever you can. And in a section that could be headed "Special Skills," you could announce your levels of proficiency in various languages.

10. EARLY RETIREE

There are many occupations from which workers traditionally retire at an age far younger than 65 and then seek new jobs. Some of the most common occupational categories include teachers, police, and people in the military. Often these workers have difficulties writing resumes because they don't know how to handle their first careers when they are applying for positions in their new career field.

Like those who are changing careers (see above), people beginning second careers need to "build bridges" for prospective employers between their first careers and the jobs they are applying for after retirement. Generally these are people with a number of skills and well-established work habits. They can be of great value to employers. Their challenge is to demonstrate how their skills and experiences can benefit the employers.

STRATEGIC MARKETING 20

THINKING LIKE AN EMPLOYER

"Strategic Marketing" is a concept that has swept across the business world in the last few years. It's a concept that should be studied by everyone who is looking for a job. Sometimes known as "Targeted Marketing," the idea is so simple that it sounds like common sense. Here it is in a nutshell: Find out what a group of people wants; create (or modify) a product that satisfies that group, and then sell the product to the targeted group by demonstrating that it has exactly the features they want. It makes sense, doesn't it? And it won't surprise you to find out that it works too!

THE CASE OF GENERAL MOTORS

Before we look at how strategic marketing principles can be applied to your resume and cover letter, let's see how they work in business. General Motors provides us with examples of failure and of success. It is well known that General Motors began to experience declining car sales in the 1980's—a decline that reached crisis proportions in the early 1990's. However, the corporation employed market researchers, before and during the crisis, who assured management that there were people who wanted the kinds of cars that General Motors was producing.

At the risk of oversimplifying, it turned out that people did say that they were interested in GM cars, but when they actually went out and bought (or leased) a new car, they found a better combination of features and value in cars from other manufacturers. They bought those cars instead of buying GM cars.

The researchers were asking the wrong questions and General Motors was producing cars the wrong way. The researchers wanted to know what potential customers thought about the cars that were already being produced by GM. They weren't asking what appealed to these same prospective buyers when they looked over the cars produced by the competition. As a consequence, they continued to produce cars that were very similar to the cars that they had produced in the past—and buyers slowly defected to buy cars that better met their changing needs.

"A NEW KIND OF CAR COMPANY"

At the very same time, General Motors was developing "a new kind of car company," as it was called in advertising campaigns—the Saturn Corporation. One of the reasons that this new division was seen as such a radical departure for GM was its "new philosophy" of car design. Instead of copying cars that were already being produced, the Saturn designers took an approach that was unprecedented at GM. They found out what features people wanted in cars, what they liked about other cars, and how much they were willing to pay. Only then did they begin to design new cars.

As their designs progressed, the designers asked prospective buyers what they thought of the designs. Not surprisingly, when Saturn produced its first cars there was a market ready and waiting for them. The idea of finding out what people want to buy and then building a product that has the features that people want may not sound revolutionary, but it was earthshaking for the largest corporation in the United States.

THE CONNECTION BETWEEN GENERAL MOTORS AND YOUR RESUME

What is the connection between designing new cars at General Motors and designing your own resume? Well, there are several parallels. As you probably know by now, resumes haven't changed much in content over the years. They may look different now (just as today's cars look different from yesterday's), but that is largely due to the widespread availability of computers and advances in desktop publishing technology. Beyond appearances, the information—and even the organization of the information on the page—really hasn't evolved very far (just as the chassis—the structure underneath the car—hasn't evolved on most American-made cars).

This is astounding when you realize that employers have been complaining for years that they aren't able to obtain the kind of information they want from traditional resumes. Like the car buyers we saw above, employers report that they have a number of needs when they are looking for new employees, but they find that conventional resumes don't meet all of their needs.

WHAT KIND OF INFORMATION DO EMPLOYERS WANT?

Here are some of the questions that employers try to answer when they are evaluating prospective employees:

"What has this person done in the past?"

"Does this person have the skills to do the job I have available?"

"What has the candidate accomplished in previous jobs?"

"What kind of contributions can I expect in the future from this person?"

"What is this person really like?"

"Will this person fit in with the team I have now?"

"How much training will be required?"

"How quickly can this person learn?"

"Will this candidate be willing to work hard and put the interests of the organization first?"

"Will this person bring in more money than I will have to spend on training and wages?"

DESIGNING A BETTER PRODUCT: YOUR RESUME

Traditional resumes answer a few, but only a few, of these questions. But these questions reveal some of the concerns of your "target market": the employers whom you will contact in the hope of being offered a job. When you are writing your resume, you are not just another job seeker. You are, in fact, a "product designer." Your challenge is to design a "product" that the "market" will buy. In plain language, you have the opportunity to create a resume that satisfies more of an employer's wants and needs than the resumes that are submitted by your competitors in the job market. With a better product, you have a better chance of success in the marketplace—in this case, with a targeted resume you have a better chance of being invited in for an interview. As you know, resumes (and cover letters) get interviews, and interviews get jobs!

The worksheets you have completed throughout this book provide the basis for your targeted resume. As you assemble the pieces into a whole resume, keep in mind the questions above. Employers want to know about your skills, especially the ones that are relevant to the job and to working as part of a team. They want to know "the real you," the elements of your personality that we have labeled "personal qualifications." They want to know what you have accomplished, with a special emphasis on how you might have reduced costs, increased income, boosted productivity, streamlined work, found new approaches—or just what you have achieved in your work life (and in your life outside work too, since your achievements there often show initiative and an ability to manage time effectively). This is why we emphasized these factors at the beginning of the book.

In addition, employers want to know how you can perform the functions of the job. One way to demonstrate your abilities is to create a resume that recognizes the kinds of skills that are required in the position you want. You can do this in a "skills" section or in the descriptions of previous experience (if it is closely related), or you can simply state that you can perform the tasks of the job. It is surprising how few people remember to address in their resumes (and in their cover letters) the specific skill and knowledge requirements that employers hope they will have. Straightforward statements like "Skilled in..." or "Qualified to perform..." or "Trained to..." should show up routinely on resumes, but are rarely included. The specifics that follow these phrases will vary with the positions you are applying for, but remember to address these issues head-on in your resume and in your cover letter too.

DOING "MARKET RESEARCH"

If you are unclear about the needs of employers in the job areas you are pursuing, you can do what product designers do—market research. You can look at "want ads" and printed job descriptions to understand some of the requirements and you can study the list of general concerns above. You can talk to people who are already in the kinds of jobs you are hoping to get. You can even speak with employers themselves, with a technique known as "information interviewing." (See the list of books in Chapter 22 for an explanation of this technique.)

APPLYING STRATEGIC MARKETING PRINCIPLES TO YOUR RESUME

"Strategic Marketing" is not a secret science. It's not even a very complex concept. Anybody can use its basic principles to write better resumes—resumes that answer an employer's wants, needs, and concerns. Put yourself in the employer's position. Spend a few minutes on the other side of the desk and pretend that you are doing the hiring. What would you be looking for in a candidate? You might even make a list of the qualifications you would want if you had to fill that vacant spot in the organization.

Now put yourself back on the side of the desk where you hope to be sitting during your job interview. What can you say about yourself that addresses the concerns you had when you played the employer? Those are the answers that you can turn into statements on your resume and in your cover letter. That is "Strategic Marketing"—knowing your market and selling to it. No one is in a better position to be a target marketer than you are. No one knows the product better than you do. Now you are ready to design the first phase of your strategic marketing campaign—your resume.

21 | RESUME PREPARATION SERVICES

WHAT THEY ARE AND HOW TO USE THEM

In nearly every telephone directory there is a section entitled "Resume Preparation Services." These businesses can be very useful, but the services they offer can vary greatly. Services range from just plain word processing (typing a finished resume that you bring in and giving you back a computer-generated "original" that you can have printed or copied) to a thorough consultation with an adviser who creates a resume for you after your first visit and then reviews it with you during a follow-up visit. There are many variations between these two ends of the spectrum.

If you have used this workbook and completed the worksheets, it is unlikely that you will need a thorough consultation with a trained adviser, unless you have trouble assembling your resume in the best possible way or have encountered problems in completing some of the worksheets. However, it is always helpful to get professional opinions, and a good adviser should be able to give you useful advice whenever you think you need it.

Because services vary so widely, it is important to know what you want and it is equally important to clarify what your local services offer. Most of your questions about resume preparation services can be answered over the phone, so "shopping around" should be pretty easy. The list of questions that follows will provide you with some ideas for the kinds of questions you might ask, but you will probably want to make your own list before you start making calls.

SOME QUESTIONS TO ASK OF RESUME PREPARATION SERVICES

1. What services do you offer?

2. Would you describe each service in detail?

3. To what extent is each service personalized to me?

4. Do all of the resumes you prepare look pretty much alike?

5. Do the resumes you prepare include personal skills, personal qualifications, and accomplishments?

6. What is your usual process in preparing a resume?

7. How would you work with me?

8. In what ways do I have input into the resume that you produce for me?

9. What if I don't like the resume that you produce?

10. Do you have a variety of sample resumes that I can look over?

11. What are the fees for your services?

12. What additional charges might there be?

13. When can I schedule an appointment to meet?

14. How soon after that appointment can I expect to see a prepared resume?

15. Are you able to provide the names of clients of yours whom I could call as references?

If you don't find the kind of resume consultation service you need in your own community, you can work by mail directly with the author of this book. You can describe your specific needs in a note or request a brochure that details the services that are available. Write to: Ray Potter, Box 12, Hopewell, NJ 08525.

22 SUGGESTED READING

THE JOB SEARCH

What Color Is Your Parachute?, Richard Bolles, Ten Speed Press

The Complete Job Search Handbook, Howard Figler, Henry Holt and Co.

Go Hire Yourself an Employer, Richard Irish, Doubleday

Guerrilla Tactics in the New Job Market, Tom Jackson, Bantam Books

Mastering the Hidden Job Market, Tom Jackson, Random House

COVER LETTERS

Cover Letters That Knock 'em Dead, Martin Yate, Bob Adams, Inc.

JOB INTERVIEWS

Sweaty Palms: The Neglected Art of Being Interviewed, H. Anthony Medley, Ten Speed Press

SAMPLE RESUMES 23

On the following pages you will find nearly fifty sample resumes. All are based on the resumes of real people. (However, their names, addresses, phone numbers, names of employers, and dates have been changed.) There are many ways to use these sample resumes to improve your own resume. Here are some suggestions on what to look for when you study the resumes that follow:

1) Organization. Examine how each resume is organized. Take a look at the overall structure. Remember that key "selling points" should be near the top of each resume, just as your selling points should be at the top of yours.

2) Phrasing. Although you won't find a whole resume here that you can use as your own, you may find specific phrases that can help you express a skill or accomplishment or personal qualification.

3) Design. There is no single "look" that a resume must have. There are a number of resume designs in these samples. One of them may reach out and grab you, or you might want to incorporate several different component parts when you design your own.

4) Occupations. It's a myth that all resumes in a certain occupation look alike and use the same phrasing. However, you might want to examine how other people in your field have presented themselves in their resumes. But don't restrict yourself to just one occupation. Look at several before you decide how you want to present yourself in your own.

5) Problems. Many of the people whose resumes appear here had to solve problems, perhaps the same problems you face as you put together your own resume. Look through these samples to see their solutions. Check the notes at the bottom of each resume, since these comments often point out problems and solutions.

Take your time as you browse through the sample resumes. You can learn a lot from them!

INDEX TO SAMPLE RESUMES

"BEFORE" RESUME

Melinda Dalessio
19 Westfield Ave.
Hartford, CT 06112
(203) 846-2291

Career Objective
To obtain a teaching position at the elementary level.

Education
University of Hartford, Hartford, CT
Graduate-Level Teacher Certification Program, Pre-K through grade 8
with a focus on Whole Language
Graduation and Certification, May 1993

University of Massachusetts, Boston
B.A. English 1989

Professional Experience

Hartford School District, Hartford, CT
March, 1993-May, 1993, Jefferson Elementary School, Hartford, CT
Student Teacher Internship
* 14 weeks full-time teaching 3rd Grade

January, 1992-February, 1993, Hartford School District Certified Substitute K-6
* Substituted K-6 all levels

Sept. 1991-January, 1993, Jefferson Elementary School Classroom Volunteer
* Volunteered in both kindergarten and 6th grade classrooms

Summer, 1991, First Presbyterian Church of Hartford, CT
Storytelling Workshop
* Volunteer Storyteller for Senior Citizens at the Church Senior Center

Work Experience
August, 1989-August 1990, Carousel Fashions, Boston, Mass.
* Assistant Manager

1985-present, seasonal, Dalessio Travel, Bristol, CT
* Administrative Assistant

Sept. 1990-August 1991, Limited Express, Hartford, CT
* Sales Associate

Note: This resume doesn't tell an employer very much about what Melinda has
to offer. It issimply a chronicle of what she has done in the past.

"AFTER" RESUME

MELINDA DALESSIO
19 Westfield Ave
Hartford, CT 06112
(203) 846-2291

CAREER OBJECTIVE
To obtain a teaching position at the elementary level.

SKILLS
- Teaching children reading, writing, and thinking in a variety of subjects
- Working effectively with groups of children as well as other teachers
- Managing time effectively
- Maintaining order and helping children resolve interpersonal conflicts
- Giving clear directions

PERSONAL QUALIFICATIONS
- Patient
- Able to work cooperatively as part of a larger unit
- Good with children
- Good with parents
- Able to pay attention to several tasks simultaneously

PROFESSIONAL EXPERIENCE

Student Teacher Internship - Jefferson Elementary School, Hartford, Connecticut
(March 1993 - May 1993)
- 14 week full-time position teaching 3rd Grade

Certified Hartford School District Substitute Teacher K-6
- Substituted K-6 levels (January 1992 - February 1993)

Classroom Volunteer, Jefferson Elementary School (September 1991 - January 1993)
- Volunteered in both Kindergarten and 6th grade classrooms

EDUCATION
University of Hartford, Hartford, CT
Graduate-Level Teacher Certification Program,
Pre-K through Grade 8 with a focus on Whole Language
Graduation and Certification, May 1993

University of Massachusetts, Boston, MA
B.A., English 1989

My complete credentials are on file in the Office of Educational Placement at the University of Hartford. They can be forwarded at your request.

Note: Here Melinda "comes alive." She speaks directly to the needs of an employer and stresses what she has to offer.

"BEFORE" RESUME

Helen Bueller • 29 Oldbridge Road • Warwick, MA 01364 • (617) 973-3662

EDUCATION:

B.A. University of Massachusetts, Boston 1993
Major: Speech and Communication

EMPLOYMENT:

Community Head Start, Warwick, MA
Assistant Teacher, Summer 1991

Central States Sports Schools, Warwick, MA
Softball instructor in girls' sports camp, Summer 1990

INTERNSHIP:

Morris-Bradshaw Public Relations, Boston, MA
Student Intern in public relations firm, Summer 1992

VOLUNTEER EXPERIENCE:

Citizens for Christine Powers, Boston, MA
Student volunteer in campaign of state senate candidate,
October 1990

COLLEGE EXPERIENCE:

University of Massachusetts, Boston, MA
Tour guide leader, 1990 - 91, 1991 - 92, 1992 - 93
Student Activities Council
Vice-President, 1992 - 93
Membership Committee, 1991 - 92

Note: In this "Before" resume, Helen overemphasizes positions and dates. She tells very little about her qualifications or accomplishments. She looks like thousands of other recent graduates.

HELEN BUELLER

29 Oldbridge Road
Warwick, MA 01364
617-973-3662

Qualifications

— Recent college graduate with solid liberal arts education.
— Excellent communicator, in person and in print.
— Strong public relations experience from summer jobs.
— Learn quickly. Understand office procedures. Very organized.
— Complete assignments on schedule. Consistently meet deadlines.
— Eager to apply my skills and make a contribution to my employer.

Education

B.A. University of Massachusetts, Boston, 1993
Major: Speech and Communication

Awarded Abigail Rice Award for Student Leadership at graduation

Accomplishments

— Wrote more than 25 press releases for large public relations firm.
— Wrote more than 10 press releases for candidate for state senate.
— Coordinated assembly and distribution of press kits, with average issue of 2500.
— Conducted phone surveys and campaigns, with totals of 500 - 1000 calls.
— Led guided tours of college campus for prospective parents for three years.
— Elected to student body offices junior and senior years.
— Assisted in Head Start program. Personally taught and cared for 10 children.
— Coached 25 high school athletes in nationally recognized softball camp.

Employment

— Morris-Bradshaw Public Relations, Boston, MA
— University of Massachusetts, Boston, MA
— Citizens for Christine Powers, Boston, MA
— Community Head Start, Warwick, MA
— Central States Sports Schools, Warwick, MA

— Proficient in WordPerfect, working knowledge of Xywrite.
— Experienced in "mail merge" functions on IBM and Apple Computers.

Note: In this "After" resume, Helen drops most dates and concentrates on her qualifications and accomplishments.

Vernon Quennell

140 Iroquois Avenue Kokomo, IN 46901 (317) 987-1450

OBJECTIVE:

A position in the travel industry

EXPERIENCE:

Travel Counselor

Responsible for high volume travel arrangements for Diners Club card members worldwide. Annual revenues from arrangements for my clients exceeded $275,000. Used strong problem-solving skills in a diplomatic way. Kept up knowledge of tour packages. Developed expertise in fitting general packages to specific needs of clients.

Diners Club Travel Related Services, Inc.

Bowie, MD

10/89 - 12/91

Temporary Office Positions

Action Temporary Services

Kokomo, IN

7/92 - Present

QUALIFYING SKILLS:

- Knowledge of domestic and international travel reference materials.
- Skills in public relations: able to network within community to create high visibility.
- Supervisory skills: able to give clear, concise directions and oversee their implementation.
- Able to prepare sales reports and necessary agency documentation.
- Skilled in bookkeeping procedures.
- 96% PNR accuracy, 96% on the Sabre Proficiency Test, 97% monitor accuracy.

EDUCATION:

College of Travel and Tourism, Cocoa, FL. Diploma, August 1989

Lake Forest College, Lake Forest, IL. Major: Business and Communications
Attended 1987-1989

Willing to travel/relocate

112   Note: In this resume, Vernon stresses his experience and skills in the travel industry. His other resume emphasizes his office skills.

Vernon Quennell

140 Iroquois Avenue Kokomo, IN 46901 (317) 987-1450

OBJECTIVE:

A position as administrative assistant or executive secretary

QUALIFYING SKILLS:

- Experienced in a variety of office settings.
- Proficient in the use of numerous software packages, including WordPerfect, Xywrite, and Word for Windows.
- Able to complete complex assignments on tight deadlines.
- Skilled in interpersonal relations, on the telephone and face-to-face.
- Extensive knowledge of travel planning.
- Competent in bookkeeping and basic accounting.

EXPERIENCE:

<u>Assistant to the President</u>
  Oribtron Industries
<u>Assistant to Director of Marketing</u>
  Chromalux, Inc.
<u>Executive Secretary</u>
  Betacom Communications
<u>Executive Assistant</u>
  Woodruff Transportation

All positions were of short duration, obtained through Action Temporary Service, Kokomo, IN (7/92 - Present)

Travel Counselor, Diners Club Travel Related Services, Bowie MD
(10/89 - 12/91)
Responsible for travel arrangements for Diners Club members worldwide.

EDUCATION:

Lake Forest College, Lake Forest, IL
Major: Business and Communications
Attended: 1987 - 1989

College of Travel and Tourism, Cocoa, FL
Diploma, August 1989

Note: In this resume, Vernon highlights his skills and experience in office positions. His other resume is focused on travel.

KARL BOYTON
4 Plower Drive
Somerville, MA 02145
(508) 892-2312 Office
(508) 892-4213 Ans. Service

CAREER SUMMARY

Over 15 years experience maintaining and repairing Air Conditioning, Refrigeration and Commercial Electrical Products. My experience, combined with knowledge gained from running my own business, can contribute to any maintenance program or organization.

EMPLOYMENT HISTORY

Owner/Operator, BOYTON SERVICE COMPANY, Somerville, MA   (10/89-Present)

Responsible for the day to day operations of a successful commercial and residential air conditioning, heating and electrical repair and installation company.

- Manage three employees
- Ensure company profitability
- Oversee sub-contractors (up to 15 per year)
- Purchase, install and repair commercial kitchens for hospitals and restaurants
- Repair and sell used electrical equipment with quality service

Manager, Maintenance and Repairs, FRIENDLY'S ICE CREAM PARLORS   (10/86-10/89)

Sole individual responsible for maintaining refrigeration, air-conditioning, electrical equipment, plumbing and heating for 10 Friendly's franchises throughout region.

- Hired sub-contractors
- Purchased equipment and parts amounting to $40,000 to $50,000 per year
- Oversaw sub-contractors during the building of new locations and repair of existing locations

HVAC "A" Mechanic, DIGITAL EQUIPMENT CORPORATION   (2/84-10/86)

Responsibilities involved the maintenance and repair of various chillers, compressors, motor control stations, hot water and steam heating systems, exhaust hoods for laboratory use, cooling water towers, pumping systems (electric and steam turbine).

- Maintained and repaired 10 Edpack computer room coolers and 19 microprocessor controlled constant temperature chambers
- Diagnosed electronic, electric and pneumatic control systems, air balance and calibration of VAV equipment, Powers 600 computer system and boiler maintenance
- Supervised up to six workers when required

SEE NEXT PAGE

114

KARL BOYTON

HVAC Mechanic, BOSTON MEDICAL CENTER   (4/82-2/84)

Responsibilities included the maintenance, repair and installation of various chillers, pneumatic equipment and controls, air compressors, vacuum pumps, commercial refrigeration, heating systems, water tower, water pumps and a domestic hot water system

- Performed arc and gas welding, brazing, blueprint reading and pipefitting
- Troubleshot wiring problems and various related maintenance jobs

HVAC Installer, YANKEE MANUFACTURING COMPANY   (8/81-4/82)

Responsibilities included installation of heaters (gas and oil), air cleaners, air conditioners, full conversions, duct-work, and thermostats.

- Made custom duct-work
- Bought various equipment for installation
- Performed all aspects of sheet metal fabrication

EDUCATION

MASSACHUSETTS TECHNICAL INSTITUTE, Boston, MA
September 1981-January 1982
Air Conditioning and Refrigeration

CAMBRIDGE COMMUNITY COLLEGE, Boston, MA
January 1982-Present
Air Conditioning and Refrigeration (Electrical Controls, Electronics)

SPECIAL COURSES/SEMINARS ATTENDED

Bitzer Steam Heating Seminar; Trane Centrifugal Seminar;
Chemtrol PVC Pipefitting Seminar; Black Seal Preparation Course;
Betz Chemicals Steam Boiler Seminar; Welding Course;
Honeywell Pneumatic Control Set-up and Maintenance Seminar

AWARDS

Certificate of Merit, Massachusetts Technical Institute, January 1982

Note: Karl promotes his experience by presenting his responsibilities and then highlighting key features.

SAMUEL LACROIX

144 Wiggins Ave., Apt. 2   (317) 769-8223 (car)
Elkhart, IN 46516   (317) 742-4689 (home)

QUALIFICATIONS

Sales professional, with accomplishments in sales and sales management in commercial accounts and retail establishments selling varied products.

Experienced in all phases of the sales process - - prospecting, closing sales, customer and credit follow-up.

• Able to quickly apply sales experience to new products.

• A "self-starter" and tireless worker who produces results.

EXPERIENCE

Area Manager, Commercial Division, Alta Fuels Co., Elkhart, IN (1990 to present)

Total responsibility for developing a new commercial division of independent fuel company. Responsibilities included generating prospects, selling, credit and customer service of newly originated commercial accounts.

• Established new commercial sales division

• Increased sales from zero gallons to 2.5 million gallons in six months

Area Manager, Enviro, Inc., Kokomo, IN (1985-1990)
Responsible for geographic area within commercial division of fuel company. Responsibilities included prospecting, placing orders, credit and customer service of commercial accounts.

• Built business unit from zero gallons to 6 million gallons in sales of fuel products to large commercial accounts such as UPS, Upland Dairy, and others

• Developed new sales regions in Kokomo and Elkhart

• Called on all levels of management, including VP's, General Managers, Purchasing Managers, and others

Sales Representative, A-I Chemical Products, Gary, IN (1983-1985)

Responsible for calling on new and existing accounts to place janitorial cleaning supplies, chemicals and paper products. Handled all phases of sales process

CONTINUED ON NEXT PAGE

• Exceeded sales goals on a regular basis

• Signed up more than 50 new accounts in 3 years

Route Driver/Sales Representative, Uniform Cleaning Services, Grand Rapids, MI (1980-1983)
> Responsible for calling on new and existing accounts to secure uniform cleaning services

• Received performance bonus each year

• Added more than 10 new, large-volume customers each year

Retail Store Manager, Kinney Shoes, Grand Rapids, MI (1981-1983)

> Total responsibility for all operations of retail shoe store.Responsibilities included all personnel functions, training, merchandising,budgets and expenses.

• Managed from 8 - 12 employees in several different stores

• Increased annual sales to more than $3 million in each store

Sales Agent, Mutual of Omaha Insurance, Escanaba, MI (1978-1981)
> Total responsibility for selling and maintaining insurance policies.

• Increased accounts 25% each year on average

• Established rapport with all types of clients

PERSONAL
• Can speak conversational French and some Italian

• Volunteer fundraiser for Muscular Dystrophy Foundation for more than 10 years. Have personally raised over $1 million.

• Volunteer assistant in pediatric physical therapy department of St. Xavier Hospital, Elkhart, TN

Note: Salespeople need to demonstrate their sales accomplishments. Sam does this job by job. He never attended college, so he doesn't have a section for education. He uses the "Personal " heading to show that he has a life beyond work.

ALBERT INGALLS
117 1/2 Chestnut Street
Flint, MI 48506
(313) 882-1976

OCCUPATIONAL OBJECTIVE

Experienced journeyman Pipefitter/Plumber seeks position where
varied skills can be applied.

EXPERIENCE SUMMARY

Inspect, repair, adjust, install and maintain all piping and
associated equipment in a major production plant. Ability to
trouble-shoot and repair problems with hydraulic and
pneumatic production machinery. Experience with high
pressure steam, air, gas, water, acids, chemicals and sewer
and waste treatment procedures.

Working experience on steel butt-weld pipe, stainless steel,
cast iron, saran, P.V.C., copper, black iron screwed and
sprinkler systems for fire control. Maintenance and repair of all
plumbing systems, steam heating and hot water heat both
industrially and commercially.

Practical knowledge of all power tools, pipe threading machines,
hand tools, measuring devices, burning and soldering equipment
associated with the pipefitting and plumbing trade.Expertise in the
removal of asbestos on piping and other areas (hold Michigan State permit).

EMPLOYMENT HISTORY

Pipefitter/Hydraulic
Fisher Guide Division of General Motors, Flint, MI (1/88 - present)

Residential Plumber
Plumber's and Pipefitters Union #12, Escanaba, MI (2/86-1/88)

Journeyman Pipefitter/Plumber
USX Corporation, Flint, MI (9/84-2/86)

Owner/Operator of Ingalls Plumbing and Heating, Flint, MI (7/83-9/84)

Residential Plumber, Ace Home Heating, Detroit, MI (4/79-7/83)

EDUCATIONAL BACKGROUND

Apprenticeship, Pipefitter/Plumber - USX Corporation
Four-year program - Journeyman, Certification

HVAC Certification Program - Metropolitan Community College

Asbestos Course Training - Michigan State University Extension Program

Note: Al clearly describes his skills in the "Experience Summary" and straightforwardly
shows how and where he acquired those skills.

118

CAROL LANSDOWNE
19 Cedar Crest
Wichita, KS 67205

316-932-1 749 (Office)
316-897-1 455 (Pager)
316-382-2365 (Home)

SUMMARY

Experienced attorney, member of the Bar in Kansas and Texas, with extensive work in litigation: discovery, depositions, motions, proof hearings, trials, and legal research. Skilled in matrimonial and family law, as well as commercial litigation.

EDUCATION

University of Texas at Austin
J.D., 1983, with distinction
Honors: Law Review,
Moot Court Competition

Baylor University
B.S., Psychology, 1980
Honors: Phi Beta Kappa

EXPERIENCE

Associate, Kramer and Heldref, Wichita, KS (1990- present)
Staff attorney in general law practice. Responsible for all aspects of practice.

Trial experience in Municipal Court, Superior Court, Federal Court, and Common Pleas Court.

Specialize in commercial litigation, often involving extensive research. Involved in actions worth more than $20 million since joining firm.

Staff Attorney, Holden and Calder, Dallas, Texas (1985-1990)
High-volume, metropolitan law firm, with broad general practice.

Litigation involved personal injury and commercial cases.

Handled wide range of legal activities, from real estate to wills and trusts.

Staff Attorney, Legal Aid Society, Fort Worth, TX (1983-1985)
Provided legal representation to all clients who met low-income guidelines.

Extensive courtroom experience.

Legal work in child custody, criminal law, motor vehicle, and many other areas.

PERSONAL

Volunteer Attorney, Legal Aid Society of Wichita

Near fluency in spoken Spanish

Note: Carol emphasizes her experience. She lists her education first because it is so impressive.

BARRY EVERETT • 112 Folkstone Ave. • **Decatur, GA 30035** • **(404) 642-7319**

CAREER SUMMARY
Over ten years progressive credit analysis and collection experience dealing with commercial, individual and government accounts with demonstrated accomplishments.

EXPERIENCE
<u>Major Accounts Analyst</u>
GENERAL MANUFACTURING, INC., Atlanta, GA
Total responsibility for the credit maintenance and collection of 40 + major accounts of minimum $1,000,000 net sales, including addressing problems, keeping invoices in good condition and ensuring that accounts stay within credit limits.
* Reduced over-90-day receivables by more than 50%
* Lowered account maintenance paper work by 70%
* Improved "skipped invoice" process, increasing receivables
* Maintained rapport with sales force achieving satisfactory problem resolutions

<u>Credit and Collections Administrator</u>
GATEWAY, INC., Augusta, GA
Total responsibility for credit and collections for entire accounts receivable, including making credit decisions, commission due reports and journal entries for write-offs and adjustments.
* Implemented use of Dun & Bradstreet and NACM credit decision process
* Reduced over-90-day receivables by more than 20%
* Utilized negotiation and communication skills to develop payment schedules and improve long-term business relationships with problem accounts

<u>Junior Accountant/Credit & Collection</u>
COMPUTER ASSOCIATES, Tucker, GA
Primary functions involved handling credit and collection of private sector, military and government software lease, lease/purchase and maintenance contracts.
* Conducted contract reviews assuring that commitments were within authorized limits
* Communicated with sales force to evaluate and resolve problem accounts

EDUCATION
DeKalb County College, Decatur, GA
Associates Degree in Applied Science with Major in Business

SKILLS
Working knowledge of IBM PC/Compatible hardware and software;
VAX 11-780; Altos Computer; WordPerfect 5.1; E-Mail

VOLUNTEER EXPERIENCE
Accountant, Big Brothers Association, Decatur, GA
Volunteer Driver, Meals-on-Wheels, Decatur, GA

Note: Barry has not been continuously employed, so he avoids dates altogether. This puts the focus on what he has done and not when he did it.

BENNO LIKUNEN

1779 Maple Drive, Oak Park, IL 60302
(312) 797-3535 Office
(312) 688-2315 Pager

SUMMARY: Experienced plant manager with recognized expertise in management of medical centers. Effective supervisor with a commitment to excellence.

EXPERIENCE:

Director of Plant Operations, St. Thomas Medical Center, Oak Park, IL (1985-1993)

Responsibilities and Accomplishments
• Responsible for $6 million annual budget
• Supervise 35 maintenance, power plant and biomedical engineering personnel, through an Assistant Director of Plant Operations and four supervisors. Trades include carpenters; electricians; plumbers; general mechanics; heating, ventilation and refrigeration; grounds upkeep and biomedical engineers.
• Established an in-house biomedical engineering department, realizing over $40,000 in yearly savings
• Obtained a federal grant to partially finance a new Energy Management System, resulting in savings of approximately $150,000 per year
• Installed a new incinerator with heat recovery, saving the hospital over $1 million per year
• Initiated, organized and coordinated a 12-week training program for all new maintenance personnel
• Acted as the owner's representative in all phases of construction of a $45 million addition bringing the construction to completion on schedule
Note: Medical Center merged with St. Peter's Hospital January 1, 1994

Director of Engineering and Maintenance, Dekalb Community Hospital (1980-1985)
Maintenance Supervisor, Cook County Hospital (1977-1980)
Director of Engineering, Quincey Rehabilitation Center (1973-1977)
Maintenance Supervisor, Barton Memorial Hospital (1971-1973)

EDUCATION
Graduate of Cook County Vocational Technical School
Major: Power Plant Engineering

Maintained continuing education through numerous seminars on all phases of engineering, management, design and construction, and codes and standards given by the Joint Commission on Accreditation of Healthcare Organizations, the American Society for Hospital Engineering and other state, federal and private educational agencies.

PROFESSIONAL SOCIETIES & AFFILIATIONS:
President & Trustee, Executive Hospital Engineers of Illinois
Trustee, National Power Engineers
Vice Chairman, Engineering Advisory Board of Illinois Hospital Association
Member, American Society for Hospital Engineering
Member, National Fire Protection Association

Note: Benno emphasizes his most recent job and then implies the reason it has ended.

BRANDON K. TRAMORE   415 Hollister Road
Pocatello, Idaho 83204   (208) 394-1779

CAREER SUMMARY
Over 25 years of Law Enforcement experience, attaining expert status in the areas of Domestic Violence, Crime Scene Investigation, and use of Breathalyzer.

EXPERIENCE
POCATELLO POLICE DEPARTMENT (December 1968 - Present)
Sergeant (June 1991 - Present)
* Supervised up to 48 Patrol Officers within all areas of the department
* Supervised and trained officers in Domestic Violence investigation and arrest
* Functioned as leading Crime Scene Investigator for the department
* Worked closely with State Police and County Prosecutor in the solving of crimes

Detective Patrol Officer (May 1988 - May 1991)
* Handled criminal investigations and preparation of cases for court
* Gathered facts by conducting interviews, collected evidence and observed activities of suspects for criminal cases
* Performed fingerprint classification, latent fingerprint identification and firearm identification at the crime scene

Patrol Officer (December 1968 - May 1988)
* Performed regular patrol duties during rapid growth period of the department

TRAINING AND EDUCATION
* Law Enforcement Officers Training School, conducted by the FBI, February 1993
* Idaho State Police, Department of Law and Public Safety, Breathalyzer Course, 1993
* Western States Police Institute, Police Management Course, November 1991
* Police Training Institute, "Kinesic Interview and Interrogation" Seminar, May 1990
* Idaho State Police Technical Bureau, six week, 240 hour course in Forensic Sciences, including Fingerprint Classification, Latent Fingerprint Identification, Crime Scene Photography and Criminalistics at the Special and Technical Services Section, May, 1989
* Idaho State Police, Drug Enforcement Course, 1980
* Six week resident Basic Training Police Course - Boise, Idaho, 1968

ASSOCIATIONS
Member, International, National and Idaho Identification Association
Member: Idaho Detectives Association

MILITARY
Member, United States Marines, Honorable Discharge, June 1968

Note: Brandon has only worked for one employer. He details clearly his experience and training.

CLARENCE L. INNIS
212 Holloway Ave.
Baton Rouge, LA 70816
(504) 788-3675

EMPLOYMENT OBJECTIVE
A Fleet Maintenance Mechanic/Auto Body Repair position that will utilize my professional skills.

PROFESSIONAL EXPERIENCE
Automotive Mechanic
Duties
- Repairs, overhauls and maintains foreign and domestic automobiles, vans, trucks, and diesels
- Discusses the description of the problem with the customer or reads work order
- Examines or test drives vehicle to determine nature and extent of repairs or services
- Quickly and efficiently prepares written estimates
- Applies knowledge of automotive electronics and mechanics to diagnose problems
- Employs expertise of auto body to repair damaged vehicles efficiently and effectively

Skills and Knowledge
- Meets all LA automotive mechanic and auto body repair certification requirements
- Working experience with on-board diagnostic computers
- Removes units such as engine, transmission, truck transfer case or differential
- Uses hoist, hand tools, micrometers, gauges, wrenches, machine tools and front-end alignment equipment
- Repairs and overhauls standard automotive systems such as cooling, air-conditioning, electrical, fuel, exhaust, brake, advanced electronics, front-end and steering systems
- Expertise in frame straightening, welding sheet metal, glass removal and repair, lighting systems, painting, finishing and detailing

EMPLOYMENT HISTORY

1989 - Present	Automotive Technician Avery Ford, Baton Rouge, LA
1988 - 1989	Automotive Mechanic and Body Repairman Sam's Auto Body Service, Baton Rouge, LA
1986 - 1988	Automotive Mechanic and Body Repairman C&J Auto Body, Laplace, LA
1984 - 1986	Automotive Mechanic Lafayette Toyota, Baton Rouge, LA

EDUCATION and TRAINING
Computer Diagnostics, Ford Motor Co.
ASE Certified Air Conditioning Technician
Laplace High School, Laplace, LA, Graduated 1984

Note: Clarence does a nice job of articulating his duties and skills. The emphasis on dates is intentional, to show that he has been steadily employed.

CLAUDIA TU   17 Prairie Ct.
Helena, MT 59601
(406) 762-3219

SUMMARY

Over 15 years of service to the citizens of Montana, progressing from Clerk-Stenographer to Administrative Secretary. Have received consecutive outstanding evaluations, based on efficient and effective performance, attention to detail, and high level of professionalism.

EXPERIENCE

Administrative Secretary,
Division of Environmental Protection
State of Montana

- Report directly to the assistant administrator of the Office of Statewide Operations
- Provide all secretarial services to the assistant administrator
- Collect and assemble information required for management reports and meetings
- Maintain appointment calendar
- Organize meetings as directed
- Prepare correspondence for signature of supervisor
- Monitor payroll time reports with office
- Communicate regularly with key personnel in other state offices
- Provide supervisor with status reports on selected projects throughout the state

Previous positions with the State of Montana include Clerk-Stenographer, Senior Clerk-Stenographer, and Principal Clerk-Stenogrpaher. Career began as Clerk-Typist in private industry.

**SKILLS AND
ACCOMPLISHMENTS**

- Proficient in use of Microsoft Word on Macintosh computers
- Organized statewide three-day meeting on the topic of "Clean Water 2000." More than 75 people attended.
- Served as co-chairperson for United Way campaign in the Division of Environmental Protection. Raised over $200,000, a 5% increase over previous year.

EDUCATION

- Enrolled in Associate of Applied Science degree program in Business, Community College of Helena
- Have earned 42 out of 48 credits required for graduation, while working full-time
- Have participated in 12 professional seminars offered by the State Department of Personnel during the last 10 years.

Note: Claudia thought she was, in her words, "just a secretary," until she completed the worksheets that led her to this resume!

DANIELLE KING
8 Brockton Road
Bar Harbor, ME 04609
(207) 699-3821

CAREER OBJECTIVE: Restaurant Management

WORK EXPERIENCE:
>   The Laughing Mermaid, Bar Harbor, ME
>   High-volume restaurant and night club in affluent tourist area.

General Manager
- Supervised all aspects of operation of 200-seat dining room, night-club, kitchen and banquet facilities, including budgets, personnel, purchasing and cost control.
- Created and implemented staff training programs in all positions which resulted in consistent increase in business during my tenure through improved service.
- Coordinated various employee functions to maintain high morale and encourage group cohesiveness, which played a major role in continuous reduction of turnover.
  11/91 - Present

Operations Manager
- Directed operation of high volume night-club (capacity 300), including inventory management, personnel, purchasing and staff scheduling.
- Designed and executed all facets of marketing plan, including newspaper, radio and in-house advertising.
- Organized all promotions for night-club and restaurant, including bands, pageants, live radio broadcasts, special events and holidays.
  6/90 -10/91

EDUCATION:
>   B.A., Economics/PublicAdministration, 1992
>   University of Maine, Orono
- Member of the National Honor Society in Economics (Omicron Delta Epsilon)
- Member of the National Honor Society in Spanish Language (Alpha Mu Gamma)
- Dean's List - Fall 1990, Fall 1991

VOLUNTEER WORK:
>   Founder and organizer of annual Bar Harbor dinner dance for American Cancer Society since 1991

REFERENCES: Available upon request.

- Fluent in Spanish
- Willing to relocate nationally or internationally

Note: Danielle began working full-time before she graduated from college. She compresses a large number of responsibilities into a compact presentation of experience.

DEBORAH HACKING
719 Flamingo Way
Naples, FL 33942
(305) 975-1637

CAREER SUMMARY
More than 15 years of progressively responsible experience in retail banking, including:
- Start-up of new branch bank
- Supervision of all aspects of branch
- Development of extensive loan portfolios

EXPERIENCE
Assistant Vice President - Manager and Commercial Loan Officer
FLORIDA NATIONAL BANK, Naples, FL
- Managed $13.5 million branch from its inception
- Supervised staff of 9 employees
- Utilized cold calls, telemarketing and referrals to develop $11 million in commercial loans and $3 million in demand deposits
- Exceeded goals for business development, total branch deposit growth and expense control

Retail Banking Officer- Branch Manager
COMMUNITY BANK OF FLORIDA, Naples, FL
- Managed the largest branch office in the district with deposits of $17 million and a staff of 10 people
- Met mandate to develop community involvement and new business development

Assistant Vice President - Manager of Office and Loan Officer
THE BANK OF DELRAY, Delray Beach, FL
- Managed the 5th largest office in the system with deposits approaching $36 million and a staff of 15 people
- Established new commercial business through an officer calling program
- Administered a loan portfolio of approximately $2 million

Regional Loan Representative
SARASOTA NATIONAL BANK, Sarasota, FL
- Administered loan portfolio of approximately 50 loans totaling $7 million
- Called on existing and prospective loan customers to establish accounts
- Analyzed financial statements, prepared loan presentation and initial credit decision recommendation and maintained credit files

Commercial Credit Analyst, Manager of Commercial Note Department, Teller, Supervisor, Head Teller Positions held at banks throughout Florida.

EDUCATION
Bachelor of Science, Business; Concentrations in Accounting and Management
FLORIDA STATE UNIVERSITY, Tallahassee, Florida

Note: Deborah held some of these positions for a very short time. However, by dropping dates and concentrating on her accomplishments, she has created an impressive resume.

Emily F. Roy
240 Gallivan Boulevard
Dorchester, MA 02124
(617) 872-3439

CAREER OBJECTIVE: A position in Corporate Accounting

HIGHLIGHTS:

✓ Earned 3 promotions in less than 5 years.

✓ Due to excellent performance, promoted to 3 positions that require a Bachelor's degree.

✓ Received Quality Award for work performed in organizing Corporate Quality Conference.

✓ Invited to join inter-company Accounting Procedures Quality Action Team that formulated procedures for post-merger transfers between business units.

✓ Taught computer packages such as Lotus, Easytrieve and Displaywrite to subordinates.

✓ Computerized daily worksheets and reconciliations previously perfomed manually.

✓ Computer experience includes: Lotus, DOS, Easytrieve, TSO, MSA, MacCormick & Dodge, Telegraf and Harvard Graphics

EXPERIENCE:

Data General, Boston, MA

    Accounts Payable Supervisor 11/91 - Present

        Supervised revitalization/reorganization of Accounts Payable Department. Implemented new procedures and controls.

        Upgrade staff skills; retrain personnel for more efficient and productive operations.

John Hancock, Inc., Boston, MA

    Trust Accounting Department Accounting Clerk (Temporary) 9/91 - 11/91

Massachusetts Transportation Authority, Boston, MA

    Accounts Payable Department Processor (Temporary) 6/90 - 9/91

Chemtel Corp., Weston, MA

    Corporate Accounts Payable Supervisor 10/85 - 6/90

        Supervised staff of 15-19 in processing payment of 161,000 invoices plus 72,000 expense reports for a total of $890 million annually.

        Developed and implemented corporate policies and procedures; oversaw system enhancements.

    Accountant I (Corporate Accounts Payable Department)

        Allocations of corporate expenses; various accounting duties.

EDUCATION: *Babson College*, Babson Park, MA
        Anticipate receiving B.S. degree - Accounting in June 1994.
        Community College of Boston
        A.A.S., Accounting, 1985

Note: Emily successfully integrates temporary work into her "experience." Nice mixture of highlights.

EVE ELIAS

128 Riverfront Drive
Apartment B-6
Independence, MO 64050

(417) 599-2811 Office
(417) 599-1712 Home

OBJECTIVE

Experienced staff accountant (C.P.A.) seeks position leading to partner status.

EXPERIENCE

Accountant, Anderson-Little, Independence, MO (7/90- present)

- Responsible for compilations, reviews and audits for various clients. Prepare financial statements, management letters, tax returns and payroll forms.
- Conduct all phases of an audit reporting directly to partner. Responsibilities include supervisory duties and administrative functions.
- Analyze brokerage portfolios through summarization of investment activity to determine return on investment.
- Represent the firm at college recruitment meetings with graduating seniors.

Accounting Intern, Guttman and Gonzales, Columbia, MO (Summer 1989)

- Member of the project team responsible for the development of a uniform chart of accounts.
- Used general ledger systems to research and summarize general ledger account activity by journal entry type.
- Assisted in the summarizing of production credit information for institutional sales offices performing directed business.
- Prepared and updated Lotus spreadsheets for analysis of profit and loss statements.

CERTIFICATIONS

Certified Public Accountant

EDUCATION

University of Missouri, Columbia, MO
Degree: Bachelor of Science, June 1990
Major: Accounting
GPA: 3.2
Honors: Dean's List
Trustees Scholarship

SKILLS

LOTUS 1-2-3, ATB, T-Value and Financial Reporting

Note: Eve provides a good example of how to present a summer internship as if it were a full-time job.

Jonathan Dietrich
1930-A Clyde Court
Norfolk, VA 23513
(804) 793-3211

OVERVIEW

Aircraft Mechanic seeking position where the experience, education and training I have gained in the military can be effectively applied in the commercial airline industry

EDUCATION

- Completed PAA Flight Safety Course
- PAA License in A & P Mechanics

Aviation Test Center, Tullahoma, TN

- Completed Primary Leadership Development Course

US Army, Fort Rucker, AL

ACCOMPLISHMENTS

- Overhauled 21 aircraft over 2 year time-frame
- Finished maintenance at least 1 week prior to scheduled delivery date
- Conducted 300 hour annual overhauls
- Functioned as Phase Team Leader
- Learned FAA flight safety rules and regulations as Non-Commissioned

Officer in charge of the Aerial Recovery Team

- Supervised 5 helicopter Crew Chiefs and 6 aircraft

EMPLOYMENT

US Army:

- Aircraft Mechanic, Saudi Arabia, Iraq, Kuwait

Operations Desert Shield & Storm

- Line Chief, Helicopter Repair, Fort Hood, TX
- Aircraft Mechanic, APO NY
- Crew Chief, Helicopter Repair, Fort Hood, TX

AWARDS

- Silver Star
- Bronze Star with Valor
- 2 Legions of Merit
- The National Defense Service Medal

Note: No dates are included here because Jon's "career" is very brief. The emphasis is on his accomplishments.

FRANCINE HANCOCK
934 Highland Street
Valdosta, GA 31602
(912) 874-931 2

CAREER OBJECTIVE: Seeking a position in Banking, Credit, or Customer Service.

STRENGTHS: Over ten years of experience in finance and banking-related fields.

EXPERIENCE:
Cashier, Valdosta State College, Valdosta, GA 1/92-present
* Cash personal checks, credit union checks, process petty cash vouchers and expense reports
* Organize and distribute bi-monthly payrolls
* Order and maintain cash balance
* Sell travelers checks, accept payments for miscellaneous accounts and refunds to company
* Summarize and account for all financial activity

Head Teller/Assistant Operations Manager
First National Bank of Georgia, Valdosta, GA 10/89-1/92
* Supervise and evaluate bank tellers
* Order and ship cash; maintain cash level in branch
* Oversee audits and safe deposits
* Buy and sell foreign currency; prepare international drafts
* Extensive customer service; MAC machine settlement

Senior Client Services Representative
Lowndes County Medical Center, Valdosta, GA 10/86-10/89
* Oversee financial services for patients and staff
* Telephone and written correspondence with physicians and other medical providers
* Monthly summary and analysis of Credit Union activities
* Assist internal as well as external auditors
* Special accounting projects as assigned by manager

Teller and Platform Assistant, First Bank of Lowndes, Valdosta, Ga 1/85-10/86
* Teller functions
* Open savings and checking accounts
* Interview potential loan candidates

EDUCATION:
B.S., Business Administration
Valdosta State College, Anticipated 1993

REFERENCES: Available upon request

Note: Francine is an adult learner presently enrolled in college. Although she has
not had high-level jobs, she articulates her responsibilities well.

GARY GOLDING
291 Bayview
Seal Cove, ME 04674
(207) 622-1974

BACKGROUND
22 years in the construction business, from
framer to carpenter to general contractor.

* Proficient in all aspects of construction
from laying out footings with transit to the finish trim
* Experienced foreman and crew chief
* Skilled cabinet and woodworking craftsman
* Qualified in all types of custom laminating work

EXPERIENCE
GARY GOLDING CONSTRUCTION COMPANY, Seal Cove, ME (1980- present)
Owner- General Contracting business. Maintain an average work force of five
employees. Handle a variety of jobs including:
• Complete renovation of 14 unit apartment building
• Renovation of retail furniture store
• Remodeling of French theme restaurant
• Remodeling and renovation of residential properties including patios, additions,
dormers, cabinets and built-in wall units
• Specialize in building custom homes from footings to the final finish trim and
cabinets
• Built 8 homes in first 10 years in my own business

BILL BREWER CONTRACTING, Portsmouth, NH (1974- 1980)
Worked as Foreman and Lead Carpenter for a general contractor specializing in
commercial and industrial construction. Examples of completed jobs are:
• A 40,000 square foot annex to a hospital building
• Total renovation of the main post office in Portsmouth
• New classroom wing of local middle school

VULCAN HOMES, Manchester, NH (1970- 1974)
Started out working for a large construction company on a framing crew, building
houses. Shortly thereafter, became foreman. Supervised the construction of large
housing projects (from 20-140 new homes).

EDUCATION
Coastal Community College
* Two years of night courses in Drafting, Design, and Blueprints

REFERENCES
Extensive references available from a wide range of clients

Note: The "background" is actually a "Qualifications Summary." Excellent use of
specific examples throughout resume.

RID NATHANSON

118-A Coventry Street • Brockton, MA • (617) 363-2971

CAREER GOAL To secure a managerial position in sales or marketing.

CAREER SUMMARY 10 years of sales, marketing and supervisory experience, with a focus on printed and packaging materials. Skills in building direct and distributor business growth.

STRENGTHS

- Outstanding track record in sales and marketing
- Highly motivated and goal-oriented
- Excellent communication skills
- Skilled sales closer

EXPERIENCE

Sales Manager, Prime Packaging, Brockton, MA (1990-1993)

- Developed $4 million in new business.
- Initiated a line of custom boxes that generated more than $1 million in sales
- Managed a sales force of 10 representatives, in plant and on the road

Manufacturers of corrugated based promotional packaging, printed index tab dividers and custom file folders.

Sales Representative, Tab Products, Providence, RI (1988-1990)

- One of the top 3 sales representatives nationally in percentage over quota: four consecutive years
- Over four years increased business from $485,000 per year to over $2 million per year (corporate average less than 10 percent per year growth)
- Conducted regional sales meetings
- Coordinated a telemarketing program that was so successful that it was adopted nationally

Sales of Printed Index Tab Dividers: retail, wholesale, printing trade

Key Account Manager, Pawtucket Paper Products, Pawtucket, RI (1985-1987)

- Created my own sales position
- Increased sales from $19,000 monthly to $58,000 monthly in two years
- Responsibilities included establishing new accounts and servicing existing accounts
- Territory encompassed Metro New York, New Jersey, Pennsylvania, Maryland and Delaware

Paper Wholesaler selling to commercial printers

EDUCATION

Bachelor of Science Degree, Management
University of Connecticut, Storrs, CT 1985

Note: The section headed "Strengths" will certainly get an employer's attention.
Ingrid describes each employer after she details her accomplishments.

132

IVAN G. INGERSOLL
22 Taylor Terrace
Brooklyn, NY 10551
(718) 694-1179

SUMMARY:
Experienced Director of Hotel Security seeks position in Western U.S.

EXPERIENCE:
The Algonquin, New York, NY
Director of Security, 6/89-Present
Developed security-related policies and procedures that have enhanced
the hotel operation
Coordinated the security arrangements for visiting dignitaries, entertainers
and executives of Fortune 500 Companies
Responsible for Security and Fire Safety training of more than 200 hotel employees
Supervise staff of 15

The Ritz-Carlton, Boston, MA
Director of Security 2/84-6/89
Instituted, as well as restructured, security and safety policies for this exclusive 4-star hotel
Coordinator and liaison with government agencies for the security of visiting
international Heads of State and dignitaries
Supervised security measures for CEOs of Fortune 500 companies and
well known public figures
Supervised and managed a department of 12 Security Officers and Timekeepers

The Helmsley Park, New York, NY
Assistant Director of Security 10/82-2/84
Hotel Assistant Manager 6/81-10/82
Security Officer 1/80-6/81

EDUCATION:
City University of New York, New York, NY
Bachelor of Science Degree, Criminal Justice

REFERENCES:
Available upon request.

Please respect the confidentiality of this resume.

Note: Ivan relies on his most recent jobs, both at well-known hotels, to secure
interviews in a new geographical region.

Jennifer Wu
Dental Hygienist
1220 Olivia Street
Key West, FL 33040
(305) 294-2291

QUALIFICATIONS:

Skilled dental hygienist. Good rapport with dentists and patients. Specialty in periodontics. Expertise in all areas of general practice dentistry. Knowledgeable in office procedures. Devoted to patient education.

EXPERIENCE:

Dental Hygienist (1990- Present) Roberta Alomar, D.D.S., Periodontist, Key West, FL
    Perform oral prophylaxsis.
    Place and remove periodontal dressings.
    Take and develop x-rays.
    Some root planing and currettage.
    Record patient histories.
    Note: Dr. Alomar is relocating her practice to Colorado in the spring of 1994.

Dental Hygienist (1988-1990) Emily Jenkins, D.D.S., General Dentistry, Columbia, SC
    Performed all dental hygienist functions in busy office.

Office Assistant (1986 - 1988) Wendall Franklin, D.D.S., General Dentistry, Chapel Hill, NC
    Part-time position in front office of solo practitioner. Learned administrative functions of office, including scheduling, billing, insurance, etc.

EDUCATION:
    College of Medicine & Dentistry
    University of North Carolina, Chapel Hill, NC
    Periodontal Certification 1988
    Dental Hygiene Certification 1986

    Appalachian State University, Boone, NC, Attended 1983 - 1985

PERSONAL:
    Volunteer hygienist at Cayo Hueso Free Clinic, Key West

Note: The "Qualifications" section is an outstanding feature of this resume. It will gain
134   a dentist's attention.

Kalle G. Xavier
41927 Skyline Drive
Topanga, CA 90290
(213) 683-2319

OBJECTIVE
Conscientious, detail-oriented recent graduate seeking position as Paralegal or Legal Secretary.

EDUCATION
A.A.S., Legal Studies, Santa Monica City College, December 1993

Dean's List; GPA 3.5

Extensive computer experience with WordPerfect 5.1 and Lotus 1-2-3

Relevant coursework includes:

Domestic Relations	Role of Legal Assistant
Survey of Torts	Courts & Trials
Practice & Pleadings	Business Law I & II
Legal Research & Writing	Wills & Probate
Real Estate Transactions	Corps. & Partnerships
Civil Litigation	Field Experience

EXPERIENCE
Intern, WomanCenter, Santa Monica, CA 9/93-12/93

- Counseled abused women on their legal rights and prerogatives.
- Accompanied clients to court.
- Interacted with judges on selected cases.

City of Los Angeles Police Department 11/87 - 11/92
Technical Assistant- Health Benefits Section

- Counseled active employees on their health benefits and plan options.
- Developed expertise in language and details of forms for various health plans.
- Extensive telephone contact and computer operations.
- Skilled in dictation and word processing.
- Promoted to Technical Assistant from Senior Clerk.

INTERESTS
Competitive rider and trainer in dressage. Have won three ribbons in regional (Western States) competition.

REFERENCES
Available on request.

Note: Willing to travel or relocate

Note: Kalle went back to school while she was employed. Like any recent graduate she emphasizes her relevant coursework and treats her internship like a job. 135

KENT ZELINKA
c/o Zelinka
2903-B Kuaui Road
Honolulu, Hl 96816
(808) 982-2873

OBJECTIVE
Naval Flight Officer seeks civilian position in organization that requires skills in management and supervision—and values capable, level-headed leadership.

MILITARY EXPERIENCE / UNITED STATES NAVY

Lieutenant, Assistant Air Department Officer
Naval Air Warfare Center, Honolulu, Hl (January 1988 - December 1993)

Responsible for air operations, aviation support equipment maintenance, computer security and staff training. Supervised 25 air traffic controllers, 15 equipment maintenance technicians, and 10 aircraft line handlers. Aviation facility's annual operating budget: $1.5 million.
- Reduced staffing by 35% with no loss in operational capability
- Reduced cost of aircraft maintenance by 25%
- Oversaw transition to new computer system

Ensign, Lieutenant Junior Grade
Naval Air Preparedness Center, Norfolk, VA (March 1985 - December 1987)

Navigator/Communicator and tactical coordinator.
Selected as Squadron Readiness Officer by superiors.
- Shaped 130 personnel into 11 fully capable aircrews ready for deployment
- Had sole responsibility for qualifying, training and scheduling all 11 crews.

Naval Flight Officer Training
San Diego, CA; Brunswick, ME; Pensacola, FL (August 1984 - February 1985)

Successfully completed prestigious 18-month training program, which included more than 50 sorties in actual flight as well as simulations in 6 different Navy and Air Force aircraft.

EDUCATION
B.S., Aeronautics & Aeronautical Engineering, 1984
University of South Carolina, Charleston, S.C.
- Naval ROTC scholarship for last 3 years of college
- Phi Eta Sigma national scholastic honor society, elected member
- Top 10% of Naval ROTC class
- Sigma Chi fraternity, Chapter President 1983-84

Note: Excellent use of "facts and figures"throughout resume. Good example of how to treat military experience as work experience.

LAWRENCE NANGLE
17 1/2 Foothill Road
Idaho Falls, ID 83402
(208) 876-1752

CAREER SUMMARY

Skilled salesperson with extensive experience in freight shipping. Strong record in acquiring and servicing new accounts. Outstanding customer relations skills.

EMPLOYMENT HISTORY

Account Manager, InterMountain Freight, Idaho Falls, ID (1992-present)
- Increased sales over 57% from 1992 to 1993
- Manage 175 to 200 accounts
- Give sales presentations to and interact with present and prospective customers
- Consistently one of top performers in region

Account Manager, Western Transport, Pocatello, ID (1990-1991)
- Managed 200 to 250 accounts in five states
- Strong in customer interaction, dealing well with clients on a one-to-one basis
- Resolved claims and service problems
- Acquired at least 50 new accounts
  Note: Western Transport closed Pocatello terminal in November 1991

Outbound Supervisor, Domino Trucking, Las Vegas, NV (1989-1990)
- Supervised dock crew to properly load road trailers
- Kept track of dock production of each crew member
- Held conferences with workers who needed training or discipline
- Held safety meetings with all workers

Inbound Supervisor, Domino Trucking, Las Vegas, NV (1987-1989)
- Supervised dock crew to properly unload road trailers
- Maintained various records of documentation for Domino and Local Teamsters Union
- Maintained proper level of discipline and order on dock at all times
  Note: This position was part-time while I completed college

EDUCATION

B.S., Physical Education
University of Nevada - Las Vegas

PERSONAL Speak conversational Spanish. Regularly use computers on the job.

Note: Larry has captured the key responsibilities of each job in his short, clear statements.

MADHURI PUNJABI   173 Maple Street
Lawrence, KS 66044
(913) 874-1998 Home
(913) 874-2382 Office

POSITION DESIRED: BOOK PRODUCTION DIRECTOR

SKILLS & QUALIFICATIONS

- *Recognized as an effective negotiator and decision maker*
- *Rewarded for consistently reducing production costs by 20-40%*
- *Thoroughly knowledgeable about book publishing and manufacturing techniques*
- *Experienced with all aspects of trade, college, reference, and art books*
- *Able to manage complex projects from initial design concept through final production*
- *Demonstrated aptitude and creativity in analyzing, researching, and solving problems*
- *Persistent, thorough, and prompt in completing projects, meeting deadlines, and staying within estimated costs*
- *Enthusiastic, energetic worker, excellent in a team setting*
- *Capable supervisor with strong people skills*

WORK EXPERIENCE
Production Manager
University Press of Kansas, Lawrence, KS 1989 - present

- *Responsible for the entire production process for art and archaeology books, as well as other heavily illustrated books: approximately 20 titles per year*
- *Negotiate contracts and bids with overseas and U.S. suppliers, constantly evaluating their performance*
- *Prepare production budgets for every book*
- *Administer effective quality control, cost containment and scheduling in the management of complex museum quality art books*
- *Effectively negotiate purchases, often resulting in $5,000 - $25,000 in savings*
- *Develop liaisons with manufacturers, in-house personnel, editors, sales, marketing, and free-lance designers*

Production Manager, W.W. Norton, New York, NY 1982 - 1989
Reprint Manager, Basic Books, New York, NY 1980 - 1982

EDUCATION
M.A., English Literature, University of Calcutta
Certificate, Book Production, University of Pennsylvania
U.S. Citizen since 1981

Note: Terrific use of skills and qualifications, nicely blended together. Wise note about citizenship.

MARGARET EARLY

221-B Merchant Green • Ann Arbor, MI 48104 • (517) 637-9210

OBJECTIVE: A position leading to a career in finance

EDUCATION

M.B.A., Finance, University of Michigan, Expected June 1995
B.S., With highest honors, University of Minnesota, June 1990

PERSONAL PROFILE

Exposure to various aspects of business, including finance, accounting, human resources, marketing and merchandising. Special talent for using innovative and resourceful methods in problem solving, time management and planning. Adaptable, able to learn quickly. Meticulous and precise; high standards for quality of work.

PROFESSIONAL SKILLS

Management: Interviewed, hired and trained staff. Responsible for all aspects of operating retail store.

Analysis: Monitored inventory stock levels, selling and merchandise trends to make purchasing decisions and optimize business profits.

Budgeting: A nalyzed monthly department spending as related to targeted budget. Created spreadsheets to organize data and compute information for presentation.

Marketing: Coordinated monthly fashion shows and promotions which generated business and improved customer relations.

Communication: Excellent selling techniques and ability to communicate with people, as well as outstanding writing skills.

Computer: Proficient in Lotus, WordPerfect, and FoxPro. Provided spreadsheet support for various departments in Technical Operations.

PROFESSIONAL ACHIEVEMENTS

Enhanced Training: Developed a training program to enhance employee product knowledge and selling skills which was adopted by stores throughout the company. Placed 60% of my store staff into managerial positions.

Increased Productivity: Created store contests and meetings to motivate staff and maintain standards of customer service, resulting in a 30% increase in annual sales.

Improved Customer Service: Awarded "Outstanding Retailer" by Main Place Mall for excellence in customer service. Received annual Productivity Award from corporate office.

EMPLOYMENT HISTORY

Senior Assistant to Director of Human Resources, W.K. Kellogg, Battle Creek, MI
(July 1992 - Present)

Manager, Jeans Plus, Main Place Mall, St. Paul, MN (December 1990 - June 1992)
Began as clerk while in college and progressed to Assistant Manager upon graduation. Appointed manager within six months.

Note: Meg put a lot of effort into identifying and grouping her skills and achievements. The effort was certainly worthwhile.

NANCY GARCIA
8915 Saguaro Way
Maricopa, Arizona 85239
(602) 292-1714

OBJECTIVE
Seeking day-shift position in nursing

EXPERIENCE

Staff Nurse, Medical/Surgical Floor
Desert Center Hospital, Maricopa, Arizona

Staff Nurse, Oncology
Desert Center Hospital, Maricopa, Arizona

Licensed Practical Nurse
Hot Springs Nursing Home, Hot Springs, Arizona

Nurse's Aide,
On-Call Emergency Care Center, Hot Springs, Arizona

EDUCATION

Enrolled in R.N. Certificate Program
Maricopa Community College

Associate's Degree in Nursing
Maricopa Community College

Licensed Practical Nurse Certification
Hot Springs Area Education Center

PERSONAL

President, Parent-Teacher Association, Hernando Soto Elementary School
Volunteer, American Cancer Society, Southern Chapter
Assistant Scoutmaster, Girl Scout Troop #153

REFERENCES

Angelina Hernandez, Nursing Supervisor, Hot Springs Nursing Home (602) 791-1812

Evelyn Katonah, M.D., Director, On-Call Emergency Care Center (602) 864-8227

Fay Ohnuki, Principal, Hernando Soto Elementary School (602) 793-2318

Note: Here is a working mother, who has worked both full-time and part-time and gone back to school. Dates would only be confusing. She works in a field that requires references.

ORLANDO TITUS
II Nottingham Drive
Duluth, MN 55807
(218) 892-9312

CAREER SUMMARY:

More than 10 years of experience designing and implementing user friendly software applications for laboratory process control, data acquisition, data analysis and data display on large scale projects. Work with extreme accuracy under pressure.

HARDWARE EXPERIENCE:	VAX Family, SUN Workstations, Gould S.E.L.
OPERATING SYSTEMS:	VMS, UNIX, MPX
LANGUAGES:	FORTRAN, C, IDL
SOFTWARE:	INGRES, SQL

WORK EXPERIENCE:

Applications Software Engineer, Physical Systems, Inc., Duluth, MN 1985 - present
Responsible for the design, implementation and maintenance of software applications using real-time control, data acquisition, data analysis and graphics for major physics projects measuring extreme densities and temperatures.

- Interfaced with end-user physicists, hardware engineers and systems programmers from initial requirements, design and implementation through maintenance and enhancements
- Served as Engineer-in-Charge to field questions and problems of physicists during experiments.
- Diagnosed and solved hardware and software problems
- Trained users in software applications
- Provided orientation and support to contract programmers

Programmer/Analyst, Southwest Oil Services, Durango, CO 1980 - 1985
Primary duties involved the design and implementation of software used in oil exploration .

- Designed and implemented database and graphics programs used by management and scientists as their major software tool
- Designed and implemented process control software of automated test systems measuring spectral responses of photomultiplier tubes under computer controlled conditions

EDUCATION

Bachelor of Science, University of Arizona, Tucson, AZ 1978
Major: Computer Science
Minor: Earth and Environmental Sciences

PERSONAL

- Worked my way around the world on oil tankers after graduating from college
- Volunteer computer science teacher in local school district's "Professionals in the Classroom" program

Note: The use of technical jargon is to be expected from a software designer.

Quentin C. Goodman

319 Greenleaf Road • Fort Wayne, IN 46804 • (812) 594-2312

OBJECTIVE:

Fitness counselor in a corporate facility where experience in the health field and
human sciences will be utilized by an employer to enhance and contribute to corporate goals.

PERSONAL PROFILE

Experienced in fitness environment; skilled in customizing general programs and equipment to the needs of individuals. Self-directed with proven leadership and decision-making skills, as well as ability to learn fast and follow directions. People skills with strong ability in written and oral communication as well as one-on-one and group instruction. Organized and detail-oriented; accustomed to handling diverse responsibilities with effective analytical, planning and management techniques.

PROFESSIONAL SKILLS

Instruction: Created and instructed an aerobic interval training class which encompassed five pieces of fitness apparatus to improve cardiovascular fitness.

Diagnostic Testing: Interacted with cardiac diagnostic team of major medical center. Experience included exposure to stress testing, echocardiographic analysis, and exercise prescription.

Communication: Lectured corporate staff in wellness-oriented subjects such as lower back care, nutrition and hypertension.

Management: Supervised daily activities of Fitness Center including maintenance of equipment, administrative tasks, and interfacing with office and medical staff.

Organization: Involved in establishment of NCR Fitness Center, which entailed designing promotional material, field testing, supervising and evaluating performance of participants.

Planning: Coordinated various activities such as ticket sales, correspondence, paperwork and training of crew members necessary in the implementation of a major promotional event. 40,000 people attended.

EDUCATION

B.S., Corporate Fitness, Wayne State University, September, 1987 to May 1992.
Related courses: Anatomy & Physiology I & 11, Exercise Physiology, Kinesiology, Nutrition, General Biology I & 11, and Fitness in Business & Industry.

EMPLOYMENT HISTORY

Fitness Center Supervisor	NCR Corporation
May 1992 to August 1992	Manufacturing Firm
Fitness Assistant	Pro Fitness
Internship - May 1991 to August 1991	Corporate Fitness Consulting Firm
Cardiac Rehabilitation Assistant	St. Thomas Medical Center
Internship - May 1991 to August 1991	Cardiac Rehabilitation Unit

Note: Willing to relocate nationally and internationally.

142   Note: "Personal Profile" mixes skills and qualifications, while "Professional Skills" includes accomplishments. An excellent resume by a recent graduate.

RAMONA ALVAREZ, A.C.S.W.
Clinical Social Worker
1142 Wayland Ave.
Louisville, KY 40210
Office: (502) 799-3535
Answering Service: (502) 794-2996

CERTIFICATIONS   Certified Board Diplomate in Clinical Social Work, 1989
N.A.S.W. Diplomate in Clinical Social Work, 1987
A.C.S.W., 1983

EDUCATION   M.S.W., Social Casework Concentration
University of Kentucky, Louisville, KY 1981
B.A., Sociology, Berea College, Berea, KY, 1978

EXPERIENCE
Director of Clinical Services
CATHOLIC FAMILY SERVICES
Louisville, KY 1990 - present

Oversee all clinical programs including personal counseling, suicide prevention, family abuse mediation, community outreach, and substance abuse treatment.

• Supervise staff of 8 full-time and 4 part-time M.S.W. social workers
• Supervise 5 support staff and paraprofessionals
• Supervise 4-6 graduate student interns

Clinical Social Worker
Private Practice
Louisville, KY 1990 - present
• Provide psychotherapy to individuals and small groups
• Provide marital, family, and personal counseling spanning a wide range of issues.

Clinical Director
THE CRISIS CENTER
Louisville, KY 1987- 1990
• Supervised all-volunteer staff at 24-hour crisis "hotline"
• Responsible for training and scheduling staff of more than 80 hotline counselors

Previous experience includes social work positions with public and private agencies in several cities within Kentucky

PERSONAL
• Placed 3rd in 1992 10-mile "Fun Run" sponsored by Louisville Charities Council
• Volunteer coach of the "Hurricanes" pee-wee soccer team

Note: In a field where certifications and education are significant, Ramona lists these first. She focuses on her most recent experience and assumes that she will discuss her first six years of work when she interviews.

Roberta B. Nadel   433 Aspen Road   Boulder, CO 80304   (303) 797-8314

OBJECTIVE
Seeking challenging position in the field of Drug and Alcohol Counseling, Testing, Interviewing, or Research

EDUCATION
B.A., Psychology, May 1993
University of Colorado, Boulder, CO

EXPERIENCE
Volunteer, Project HELP, Boulder, CO June, 1993 - Present

Intake worker for people living with AIDS.
Includes interviewing to assess risk taking behavior, personal stability, apparent level of distress and service needs. Provide crisis counseling and crisis intervention on an as-needed basis and assist in obtaining entitlements, health care, housing and other services. Active in Buddy Program, providing companionship and social and recreational opportunities to people living with AIDS, and assist with meals program serving homebound clients.

Intern, Boulder House, Boulder, CO January - May, 1993

Counselor at general psychiatric/alcohol and drug abuse treatment facility.
Worked in Dual Diagnosis program under direction of Psychiatric Social Worker:
- Facilitated adjunctive therapy groups.
- Conducted some one-to-one counseling sessions.
- Participated in daily Dual Diagnosis Meetings.
- Attended daily General Staff Meetings.
- Completed billing and patient charting.
- Helped set up aftercare.
- Followed-up on aftercare arrangements after discharge.

INDEPENDENT STUDY
Diabetes Clinic - Boulder Medical Center, Boulder, CO. 1/93 - 5/93
Researched coping skills of adolescents with insulin-dependent diabetic mellitus and their parents. Observed patients' and families' behavior.

Rocky Mountain Psychiatric Hospital, Boulder, CO. 1/92 - 5/92
Facility treating Mentally Ill/Chemically Addictive (MICA) patients. Designed and developed interview forms for research project on treatment plans for dual diagnosis patients. Interviewed patients and staff about dual treatment plan.

Note: Here is an entire resume without paid work experience. Notice how Roberta has treated her unpaid experience.

SHERI MENDEL
84 Creek Road
Missoula, MT 59806
(406) 751 - 1953

GOAL:
Seeking part-time position as medical assistant. Special expertise in management of diabetes. Excellent interpersonal skills.

EDUCATIONAL QUALIFICATIONS:
Western Montana Community College
Medical Assistant Training Program
Graduated 1993

Montana State University
B.S., Biology, 1978

Most recent training included:

ADMINISTRATIVE:
- scheduling
- medical records management
- medical transcription
- accounting/billing
- patient relations

CLINICAL:
- medical histories
- laboratory procedures
- taking vital signs
- sterilizing instruments
- patient education

Certified Medical Assistant
Member, American Association of Medical Assistants

BACKGROUND:

American Diabetes Association
- President, Diabetes Association of Missoula (local chapter)
  Served two terms: 1986-1988; 1990-1992
- Delegate to state association from Missoula chapter, 1989-1990

- Have lectured throughout western part of state on diabetes and insulin management
- Have attended numerous workshops on diabetes
- These experiences led me to pursue education as medical assistant

PERSONAL:

Single parent of teenage diabetic child. Able to work up to 30 hours per week.

Note: Sheri has completed a training program after 15 years of working in the home and as a volunteer. Her son was severely diabetic when he was younger. Her resume makes the most of her recent training and her volunteer work.

TANYA YOUNG
11954 Silverado, Apt. 3, Phoenix, AZ 85016 (602) 493-1337

QUALIFICATIONS
Experienced sportswear and accessories buyer who has consistently exceeded sales goals. Knowledgeable in all aspects of retail clothing store operations and purchasing.

EXPERIENCE
Buyer, Sportswear
>   FASHIONS WEST, Phoenix, AZ (Corporate Headquarters) 1992 - present

Function:
• Responsible for all aspects of buying and merchandising sportswear for chain of 15 stores with annual sales volume over $4 million

Accomplishments:
• Generated a 25% increase in sportswear sales in two years
• Increased sportswear sales from 70-80% of total company's sales volume in two years
• Worked closely with manufacturers to develop exclusive merchandise for stores
• Planned, purchased for and attended new store openings
• Developed sportswear sales plans for all 15 stores

Manager
>   CAREER CORNER, Tucson, AZ 1989 - 1992

Function:
• Managed a $2 million retail clothing store

Accomplishments:
• Hired, trained and developed staff of eight
• Increased sales by more than 10% per year
• Maintained high level of communication with own staff members and upper management to ensure company objectives were met

Assistant Buyer
>   I.MAGNIN, Los Angeles, CA 1987 - 1989

Function:
• Active partner in coordinating procurement, store distribution and seasonal sales/stock plans

Accomplishments:
• Purchased more than $10 million per year in sportswear and accessories
• Projected seasonal advertising plans by determining advertisement strategies in each geographic market and determined productivity of advertisements through analysis of computerized retail buying records

EDUCATION
SYRACUSE UNIVERSITY
Bachelor of Science Degree
Retailing & Marketing
Grade point average in major: 3.6 (on 4.0 scale)

Note: Tanya outlines her function and accomplishments for her most recent jobs in a very appealing way.

Terese B. Ellermann

112 Shore Drive
Dover, DE 19901
(302) 979-6388

OBJECTIVE

A product development position which will utilize my technical design skills
in electrical engineering.

WORK EXPERIENCE

Product Development Engineer

Fluortech, Inc. January, 1992- Present

Work to develop state-of-the-art fluorescent lamp ballasts for small start-up company.
Develop products from the conceptual stage to the production level.

Responsible for:
- ✔ Circuit design and documentation
- ✔ Component specification and sourcing
- ✔ PCB Design
- ✔ UL listing procedures and quality procedures
- ✔ Resolving quality issues
- ✔ Managing six-terminal LAN system

TECHNICAL EXPERIENCE

CAD for schematics, PCB layout and auto-routing, AutoCAD
LANtastic Network OS and related hardware
Pascal, BASIC, Assembly languages for TMS320C25, 8088, 8051
PSPICE and Microcap simulation programs

EDUCATION

University of Delaware
Bachelor of Science, January, 1992
Major: Electrical Engineering

Designed Voice Recognition System using TMS320 DSP chip.
Researched speech theory and recognition algorithms for use in
assembly program. (Senior Project, January - December, 1991)

Note: Terri has had only one job, but she has clearly spelled out her responsibilities
and her technical knowledge.

ULANDA HART
7184-A Heron Parkway
Little Rock, Arkansas 72206
(501) 882-2319

OBJECTIVE   Hard-working college graduate with degree in accounting wants to make a contribution to the financial health of a bank or business.

EXPERIENCE
Little Rock Savings Bank, Little Rock, AR
<u>Bank Reconciliation Technician</u> 6/90- present
* Reconcile investor custodial accounts
* Research inquiries from mortgagors and investors regarding disbursements
* Initiate wire transfer of funds between savings bank and Federal Home Loan Bank
* Investigate foreclosure loss at loan level basis, enabling management to make proper account entry decisions

<u>Cash Technician</u> (part-time position) 1/89-6/90
* Reconciled foreclosure loss reserve accounts
* Prepared Real Estate Owned reports for presentation to Board of Directors
* Researched individual mortgage accounts
* Processed payoffs, regular installment payments and foreclosure settlements

University of Arkansas, Little Rock, AR 6/87-9/87
<u>Bookkeeper</u>, Council of Student Organizations
* Paid part-time accounting position
* Dispersed more than $500,000 in student funds
* Wrote all checks requested by more than 75 student organizations

EDUCATION
University of Arkansas, Little Rock, AR
Degree: Bachelor of Science, June 1990
Major: Accounting
Note: Self-financed 80% of cost of education

SKILLS
Lotus 1-2-3; Quattro; Paradox; Data Base 111; Wordstar: Professional Write

ACTIVITIES
National Association of Accountants (Student Member) 1988-1990
Delta Delta Delta Sorority 1987-1990, Treasurer 1989-1990
Intramural co-ed rugby team member

REFERENCES
Available upon request

Note: Ulanda makes the most of her limited experience and keeps the resume focused on accounting and finance.

UNA S. UNDERWOOD

815 Summit Road
Juneau, AK 99850
(907) 331-8956

SUMMARY

Over 5 years experience installing, troubleshooting, administrating,developing, implementing and training with IBM/PC's in a Local Area Network Token Ring Architecture and with Wang's PC's in a Wide Area Network

ACCOMPLISHMENTS

ADMINISTRATION

- Administered, planned and maintained a Local Area Network made up of IBM PS/2's on an OS/2 Token Ring
- In charge of distributing and maintaining all computer equipment for office
- Delivered, installed, and provided maintenance on networked PC's, mainframes, and software for 120 legislative district offices, eliminating the need for a $250K maintenance contract

DEVELOPMENT

- Developed interface between Auditor's office PC LAN and the Legislature's Bill Tracking and Statute Retrieval System, improving auditor efficiency
- Developed and implemented an inventory and resume database used by peer review for annual certification
- Improved productivity by developing and implementing a project management system
- Initiated enhancement of audit reports by introducing desktop publishing
- Developed and implemented a training program for in-house users

TECHNICAL

Hardware	Token Ring LAN Architecture using IBM PS/2's, Wang Systems
Software	WordPerfect, Multimate, Quattro Pro, E-Mail, Lotus 1-2-3, dBase, Alpha 4, SAS
Operating Systems	OS/2, MS-DOS, JCL

EXPERIENCE

State of Alaska, State Auditor's Office, Juneau, AK
Auditor, 12/92 - Present
State of Alaska, Office of Legislative Services, Juneau, AK
PC User Consultant, 7/89 - 12/92

EDUCATION

University of Alaska, Juneau, AK
BS in Business Administration Major: Accounting, 1989 - 1992

Sheldon Jackson College, Sitka, AK 1988 - 1989

Note: Una divides her accomplishments into three separate categories and then lists her employment history.

XAVIER FREDERICK
31275 Baltimore Pike Bowie, MD 20720 (410) 597-2279

OBJECTIVE: Seeking responsible position in corporate security. Offering
extensive experience and education.

EXPERIENCE:

Senior Correction Officer, Maryland State Correctional Facility (1993-present)
* Control Post Officer with detail of approximately 30 officers, overseeing access to four
  major areas
* Procure supplies, issue job assignments and supervise inmate workers in their assigned tasks.
* Maintain monthly payroll and rating system for employees, including weekly updates.
* Perform various other custody functions including inmate and area searches,
  maintaining discipline, and control of contraband.
* Perform investigations on inmate infractions and issue disciplinary reports
* Supervise up to three officers in conducting investigations

Senior Correction Officer, Baltimore County Youth Home (1985-1988)
* Housing Officer in charge of approximately 20 juveniles on an assigned shift
* Maintained custody and control of juveniles while also safeguarding their well-being
  and attending to their individual needs

EDUCATION:

Pursuing B.S. in Administration of Justice, Bowie State College
Degree expected, June 1994
A.A.S. Corrections, Community College of Baltimore, (1988)

MILITARY:

Operations Officer, U.S. Army, Berlin, Germany (1990-1993)
* Responsible for developing, producing, acquiring and supporting weapons systems,
   ammunition, missiles and ground mobility material during peace and war.
* Comprehensive knowledge of maintenance management, production control and
  quality assurance

Officer Candidate School, Quantico, VA
* Commissioned Officer, 2nd Lieutenant, September 1, 1990

REFERENCES: Excellent personal and professional references available upon request.

PLEASE MAINTAIN THE CONFIDENTIALITY OF THIS RESUME.

Note: Xavier's military service comes between his two jobs but he groups the related work
together and handles military service in its own section.

150

CATHERINE M. YANG

12235 34th St., Apt. 3-G
Chicago, IL 60612
(312) 674-2932 (Office)
(312) 976-7413 (Home)

SUMMARY

Award-winning copywriter
 Work effectively as team member
 Relate well to clients
 Skilled in research techniques
 Manage photographers, graphic designers, media planners,
 and production personnel
 Develop effective advertising, marketing, p.r. and positioning campaigns

EXPERIENCE

General Foods (print ads) Pioneer Audio (package design) Westside Electronics
(newspaper ads) Mita Copiers (collateral materials) Chicago City College
(magazine, newspaper, transit ads) Chicago Museum of Art (direct mail
campaign awarded first place in competition with all museums in Illinois)

EMPLOYMENT

Megacom (ad agency) Chicago, IL
 Senior copywriter
Smith, Coverdale (ad agency) Chicago, IL
 Copywriter
Clovis and Maven (ad agency) Chicago, IL
 Copywriter

EDUCATION

B.A., English, Lake Forest College, Lake Forest, IL
Participant, "Shakespeare Semester," Stratford-on-Avon, England

PERSONAL

Volunteer Director, Southside Children's Theater, Chicago
Drama coach/director at inner city theater program for disadvantaged youth

Note: Advertising-industry resumes concentrate on accounts and campaigns.
Their design can be unusual.

Anita Ramone • c/o Elite Talent Management
925 Peachtree Road • Atlanta, GA 30318 • (404) 977-3422

TELEVISION:

"Days of Our Lives": Waitress (speaking part)
"Santa Barbara": Nurse (walk-on)
"Beverly Hills 90210": Secretary (non-speaking)

NATIONAL ADVERTISING:

Atlanta Braves: Fan (close-up)
Georgia Tourism Board: Vendor (speaking)

LOCAL ADVERTISING:

15 appearances to date including 10 speaking parts. Featured parts in commercials for Peachtree Spa, Doubletree Hotels, and Calhoun Nissan.

NATIONAL FILM:

"Doc Hollywood": patient (non-speaking)
"My Cousin Vinny": courtroom spectator (non-speaking)

VIDEO:

21 appearances to date in industrial videos. Featured parts in 5 videos, including narrator for "Our Georgia: Welcome To It" produced for Georgia Tourism Board (on-screen speaking and overdubbed narration).

TALENTS:

Read and speak Spanish
Excellent with accents. Can do inflected English, with Spanish, French, and Italian accents.
Face and hands used extensively in close-ups.
Can portray numerous ethnicities
Good with children of all ages
Good with all kinds of animals
Play piano, flute, violin, viola

Can travel. Available on short notice.

Note: This is a typical resume for an actress. The focus in on "appearances." A photo accompanies the resume.

CURRICULUM VITAE

Kanesha Turner

University of Missouri   Department of English
Columbia, MO 65202   (314) 767-9734

PRESENT POSITION
Assistant Professor of English, University of Missouri, 1992 - Present

EDUCATION
Ph.D., English, University of Georgia, Athens, GA 1991
    Dissertation: "The Dark Side of The Moonstone: Tragedy and Melodrama in the Works of Wilkie Collins"
M.A., English, University of Georgia 1987
B.A., English, Spelman College, Atlanta, GA 1983
    Graduated with honors
    Distinction in senior thesis

TEACHING EXPERIENCE
Visiting Adjunct Instructor of English, Georgia Southwestern College, Americus, GA 1990 - 92
Courses included: Composition 1, Introduction to English Literature, Introduction to the Victorian Novel

Teaching Assistant, University of Georgia, 1985 - 90
Courses included: Composition, Advanced Composition, Honors Composition, Introduction to Literature, English Literature: An Introduction, The Victorians, Introduction to the Victorian Novel

ADMINISTRATIVE EXPERIENCE
Coordinator, Freshman Composition Program, University of Georgia 1988 - 90
Elected representative to faculty senate, Graduate Student Association, 1987

PUBLICATIONS
"The Dark Side of The Moonstone: Tragedy and Melodrama in the Works of Wilkie Collins," accepted for editorial review by University of California Press and University of Chicago Press
"Tragedy Meets Melodrama: Wilkie Collins and The Moonstone," 19th-Century Literature, Vol. 10, 2, Summer 1993
"Melodrama and Tragedy in Victorian Novels," published as chapter in *Teaching the Victorian Novel* (University of Minnesota Press, 1992)

LANGUAGES
French: reading proficiency, writing proficiency, speaking fluency
German: reading proficiency
Spanish: speaking proficiency

Note: This is a "vita." Kanesha is typical of a professor early in a career.
The section entitled "Administrative Experience" is a smart addition to the vita.

CARL UNWYN

120 Spur Circle
Houston, TX 77020
(713) 592-2312

SUMMARY

Offering over 12 years' experience in the Information Systems and Telecommunications industry: 5 years in technical training and 7 years directly dealing with customer support and equipment maintenance

QUALIFICATIONS

✔ Skilled teacher
✔ Experienced engineer
✔ Effective with clients, coworkers, and computers
✔ Thorough knowledge of UNISYS product line
✔ Productive in a variety of work settings

ACCOMPLISHMENTS

UNISYS CORPORATION, HOUSTON, TX
Developer / Instructor (1986-present)

✔ Responsible for the development and delivery of training for PC and Unix communications and network products
✔ Led team to develop a self-paced computer, video and text based training package which was accepted as corporate standard and used nationwide
✔ Developed and conducted more than 20 hardware classes on mainframes, mini's and PC's
✔ Developed and conducted more than 10 software classes on operating systems and applications
✔ Taught over 150 students per year in small-group training sessions.

Senior Site Engineer (1979-1986)
✔ Responsible for installation, maintenance, upgrade and repair for mainframes, peripherals and communications equipment
✔ Increased installation efficiency by 15%, leading to improved customer satisfaction and decreased company costs
✔ Supervised 3 trainee engineers prior to their permanent site assignments
✔ Employed preventative maintenance procedures to maintain on-line site effeciency of 99.5%. This resulted in one of the lowest "down time" rates of any corporate field office

PLEASE SEE NEXT PAGE

MILITARY SERVICE:

U.S. AIR FORCE (1971-1979)
Responsibilities included maintenance and repair of
airfield based and mobile communications, radar
and navigational equipment

EDUCATION

U.S. AIR FORCE Technical Training School
Associate Degree

TECHNICAL TRAINING

UNISYS Education Center, Houston, TX
✔ UNIX Communications & Networking, 1990
✔ UNIX Shell Programming, 1990
✔ UNIX System Administration, 1990
✔ Local Area Network Administration, 1988
✔ 2200/600 Engineering Class, 1988
✔ 1100/90 Advanced Troubleshooting, 1987
✔ Technical Instruction & Development, 1986
✔ 1100/60 System Maintenance, 1985
✔ Peripheral Theory & Repair, 1985
✔ U1050 - II System Maintenance, 1980

SOFTWARE EXPERIENCE

LAN   Novell Netware 286
UNIX   System V.3, Shell, C, TCP/IP, UUCP, FTP, SMTP
PC   MS-DOS, Basic, C, dBase III, Clipper, Excell 2.1,
Word Perfect 5.1, Draw Perfect 1.1, Harvard Graphics 2.1,
XyWrite III, Misc Utilities
Mainframe OS1100, ECL

HARDWARE EXPERIENCE

PC   Unisys - HT, JT, UIT, PW2 500
Communication Unisys - DCP40/20/10
Mainframe Unisys- 2200/600ES, 2200/600, 2200/400,
2200/200, 100/90, System II/Mapper 10, 1100/60,1050-II
Peripheral Unisys - Disk: 8433, 8436, 8440, 8451, 8470,
8480
Unisys - Tape: U22/24, U26/28, U30/32, Steamer
Unisys - Printer: 770-II, 776, 789

Note: Carl's resume is well-detailed and very specific. He devotes the first page to catching
attention and the second to technical specifications.

CLAUDIA BATEMAN

2319 Valencia Drive
Tustin, California 92701
Home (714) 542-5796   Work (714) 639-2710

PROFESSIONAL OBJECTIVE

Position as a Learning Disability Teacher/Consultant

HIGHLIGHTS OF QUALIFICATIONS

- Over 15 years experience meeting educational needs of special students
- Committed to equal opportunities for all students
- Capable of working in varied settings
- Collaborate well with colleagues and administration

PROFESSIONAL EXPERIENCE

ASSESSMENT

- Evaluated students using varied assessment methods including:
  - standardized and criterion instruments
  - curriculum based assessment
  - product evaluation
  - diagnostic teaching
  - student and teacher interview
  - record review and classroom observation
- Assessed students presenting a diversity of educationally handicapping conditions including emotional disturbance, all levels of retardation, autism, multiple handicaps and learning difficulties.

COLLABORATIVE PROBLEM SOLVING

- Empowered teachers to develop more effective instruction to meet the needs of an extremely diverse student population.
- Obtained support and involvement from administrative, professional and non-professional staff to identify and address instructional challenges.

CASE MANAGEMENT

- Performed approximately 100 annual reviews and reclassifications in compliance with state and federal regulations.

CURRICULUM DEVELOPMENT

- Assisted in the development of a Curriculum Guide used in the educational facilities of the Department of Human Services.
- Researched and wrote curriculum for mental health course used with students in a psychiatric facility. Course spanned 3 years and involved 300 participants. Program was submitted by Department of Human Services to the American Psychiatric Association's Achievement Awards Competition.
- Wrote Child Study Team Newsletter to share sound educational ideas and practices with teaching staff. Designed newsletter to be interactive by inviting teacher participation. Secured active involvement of 85% of staff.

WORK EXPERIENCE

1990 - Present
- Learning Disability Teacher/Consultant
- Serve as case manager for Douglas Training and Research Center and Naremore Development Center
- Perform educational assessment for 8 local inpatient and outpatient psychiatric centers
- Conduct per-case evaluations for private, public and parochial schools

1982 - 1990 Teacher, Frederick Psychiatric Hospital
- Full-time position working with students of all ages and backgrounds
- Implemented innovative peer reading program

1975 - 1982 Teacher, Special Education - various public school districts
- Experienced in T.M.R., Resource Room and Primary ED class
- Supervised para-professional assistants
- Developed reading programs

PROFESSIONAL CERTIFICATIONS
L.D.T.C. 1988
Teacher of the Handicapped 1975
Elementary Education 1975

EDUCATION
1988 University of Southern California, L.D.T.C. Certification Program
1986 University of Southern California - Course leading to Principal Certification
1982 M.A. University of Southern California, Special Education
1975 B.A. California State College, Fullerton, Major - English, Minor - Elementary Education

PROFESSIONAL ASSOCIATIONS
California Association for Learning Consultants
Council for Exceptional Children

REFERENCES
Will be furnished upon request

Note: Claudia first highlights her qualifications and experience and then details her employment and education.

Karen Trump

11921 Westend Avenue
New York, NY 10012
Apartment 3-G

(212) 979-2673

QUALIFICATIONS

Graphic artist skilled in the use of state-of-the-art technologies
Electronically "draw" images for computer animation
Create special effects in type and backgrounds for a nationally televised
home shopping service
Design storyboards on computer
Shoot, edit, and sound-edit short video footage
Utilize all traditional graphic arts in design of print materials

EXPERIENCE

<u>Video Layout Artist</u>, Electronic Media Department, Macy's, Inc.,
New York, NY (1991 - Present)
Computer graphic artist for televised home shopping service
Create still video screens (with type and images) for national broadcast
Develop and implement procedures, techniques, and formats for adapting
color catalog ektachromes to television medium
Supervise and train three computer graphic artists
Develop methods of archiving video frames
Interact with printed catalog art staff as liaison from electronic catalog department

<u>Senior Graphic Artist</u>, Consumer Catalog Department, Macy's, Inc.,
New York, NY (1988 - 1991)
Supervising layout artist for four major catalogs and twenty-eight tabloids per
year
Designed layout and type specifications
Supervised staff of three graphic artists
Interfaced with photographers and printers to ensure accurate and timely produc
tion of catalogs
Created new design formats for publication
Previous experience includes positions as layout artist and paste-up artist for
catalogs, magazines, and book publishers

TECHNICAL

Skilled in use of Macintosh computers and peripherals
Skilled in use of numerous design software packages, including PageMaker,
Studio 8, Quark Xpress, MacroMind Director, Type Styler and others
Skilled in use of Colorgraphics Art Star 3D computer and peripherals

EDUCATION

B.A., Fine Arts, New York University
Continuing education courses at Parsons Institute of Design, New York City

Note: Karen positions herself immediately with her qualifications. She has
been a graphic artist for many years but she does not indicate any dates
that might reveal her age.

Michael Mendez
119-D Coventry Lane
Surfside, CA 90743
(707) 968-4923

SUMMARY

Marketing Manager skilled in all phases of marketing, with special strengths in catalog marketing and targeted direct-response marketing.

EXPERIENCE

Marketing Manager, Allcraft Publishing, San Luis Obispo, CA
• Increased sales volume by 15% in first year
• Reduced marketing expenses by 20% in first year through better targeting of catalog mailing
• Increased catalog sales by 30% in three years
• Increased overall response rates from 4% to 8%: a 100% jump in three years

Specialty publisher of craft books, with an emphasis on handcrafts (1991 - Present)

Assistant Marketing Manager, Alessi Yarn Co.,
Los Angeles, CA (1989 - 91)
• Doubled income from direct-to-consumer marketing
• Initiated first consumer advertising campaign
• Supervised transition from black-and-white to four-color catalogs for wholesalers, retailers, and consumers

Assistant Marketing Manager, Wonderland Looms, Duluth, MN

Sales Representative, Wonderland Looms, Duluth, MN

EDUCATION

Bachelor of Business Administration
University of Iowa, Iowa City, IA
Major: Marketing   Minor: Advertising   June, 1986

PERSONAL

Volunteer tutor at La Raza Community Center, San Luis Obispo, CA
Volunteer speaker in local program: "Education Means Jobs"

Note: As a marketing manager, Mike concentrates on his tangible results in his two most recent jobs.

A SERVICE TO READERS

DO YOU NEED SOME HELP WITH YOUR RESUME?

Resumes That Get Jobs is a book that is designed to help you write your own best resume. However, it can be very useful to have professional assistance in preparing your resume. Whether you have specific questions or just want to have a trained eye look over your resume, help is available. The author of this new and expanded edition of *Resumes That Get Jobs* can be consulted by mail. If you would like help in putting together your resume or cover letter, write for a free brochure.

Send your request to: Ray Potter, Box 12, Hopewell, NJ 08525

If you have suggestions on how to improve this book, or if you want to pass along a copy of the resume you prepared after using the book, write to the author at the address above.

BOB THOUGHT THAT THE BLUE RIBBON WAS SURE
TO GET AN EMPLOYER'S ATTENTION.